James Holt Haslam

# The Mountain Meadows Massacre

Who were guilty of the crime?

James Holt Haslam

**The Mountain Meadows Massacre**
*Who were guilty of the crime?*

ISBN/EAN: 9783743395756

Manufactured in Europe, USA, Canada, Australia, Japa

Cover: Foto ©Suzi / pixelio.de

Manufactured and distributed by brebook publishing software
(www.brebook.com)

James Holt Haslam

**The Mountain Meadows Massacre**

# THE

# MOUNTAIN MEADOWS MASSACRE.

## WHO WERE GUILTY OF THE CRIME?

## AN ADDRESS

—BY—

ELDER CHARLES W. PENROSE,

*October 26, 1884.*

Also a Supplement Containing Important Additional
Testimony Subsequently Received.

GEO. Q. CANNON & SONS CO.,
SALT LAKE CITY, UTAH.
1899.

# THE
# MOUNTAIN MEADOWS MASSACRE.

WHO WERE GUILTY OF THE CRIME?

## AN ADDRESS

—BY—

## ELDER CHARLES W. PENROSE,

*October 26, 1884.*

Also a Supplement Containing Important Additional
Testimony Subsequently Received.

GEO. Q. CANNON & SONS CO.,
SALT LAKE CITY, UTAH.
1899.

# INTRODUCTION.

———

THERE is a general misunderstanding in the public mind in reference to nearly every subject connected with "Mormonism." Particularly is this the case in regard to "Mormon" doctrine on the taking of human life. It is popularly supposed that the Church of Jesus Christ of Latter-day Saints authorizes and justifies the killing of men and women for apostasy, or for any grave act in opposition to its interests. This is called "blood atonement" by unprincipled writers and lecturers who wish to deceive the public, and many people believe that this is really one of the tenets of this Church. The Mountain Meadows Massacre has been made to do active duty in the work of deception. It has been charged to the "Mormon" Church and the "Mormon" leaders so many times and in so many places that any attempt to present the facts seems almost like labor in vain. And yet to allow these falsehoods to go unrefuted appears wrong and impolitic. They should be met and overturned for the benefit of the few among mankind who prefer the truth to deception and love light rather than darkness. It was for the purpose of aiding in the correction of error concerning these subjects that the author responded to an invitation to deliver a public address in the Twelfth Ward Assembly Hall, Salt Lake City, on the subject of "Blood Atonement," and another two weeks later on "The Mountain Meadows Massacre." In the former address the doctrine of the Church on the shedding of human blood was explained and substantiated and popular errors exposed, by reference to the Church standards and the sermons of leading Elders. In the latter address the responsibility of the terrible crime committed at an early date in this Territory was traced to its true source, and numerous references were made to anti-Mormon works, and documents of unimpeachable authenticity and veracity were introduced for the first time in a public assembly. These addresses have now been published, by request, in pamphlet form, and are submitted to the world for the perusal and judgment of thinking men and women everywhere. And the blessing of the Author of all truth and light is invoked upon these simple but earnest efforts to enlighten mankind, to the end that prejudice may be dispelled, to make way for the everlasting truths which a maligned and misunderstood Church has a mission to proclaim for the salvation of man and the glory of God.

CHARLES W. PENROSE.

# THE MOUNTAIN MEADOWS MASSACRE.

THE subject upon which I have to speak this evening has attracted a great deal of attention. It has been mentioned, I think, in every part of the civilized world. Wherever our Elders have gone abroad to preach the gospel of Christ they have been met with the statement that the "Mormon" Church, with Brigham Young at its head, is a bloody church; that it not only teaches, but practices the doctrine of shedding human blood for apostasy; that there is an organization in the midst of the people called "Danites" or "Destroying Angels,"* whose business it is to kill everyone who attempts to escape from Utah, or any obnoxious person, "Mormon" or Gentile, who may come into the midst of the people. This has been denied frequently, and those who have made these statements have been challenged to the proof. The proof, of course, has not been forthcoming, because the charge is a falsehood. Still, wherever our Elders go they meet with a statement of this kind, and particularly is the cry of "The Mountain Meadows Massacre" raised against them. It is

---

* For refutation see my "Address on Blood Atonement."

claimed that that awful tragedy was performed by the "Mormon" Church, or that the "Mormon" Church is responsible for it; that it was perpetrated at the command of Brigham Young as the leader of the Church, and that it was in accordance with the doctrines of the Church.

This untruth has been repeated so many times that the world, who are not acquainted with our principles and our acts, have come to believe in a great measure that it is true. It has been proclaimed by the press repeatedly. Over and over again the Mountain Meadows massacre has been charged to the "Mormon" Church, and particularly to its former President. Ministers in the pulpit have found this a convenient weapon wherewith to oppose the Elders of the Church in the preaching of the gospel. They could not refute the arguments which they brought forth, they could not overturn the doctrines which they preached, and so stories like those I have mentioned have been told from the pulpit, over and over again, to prejudice the public mind against the Elders of the Church. Wherever the servants of God have gone to preach the gospel, the Mountain Meadows massacre has been thrown in their teeth.

Now, this evening I will endeavor to give a brief account of this terrible occurrence, and then, if possible, to trace up the responsibility for it, show who perpetrated it, who were the guilty parties, so far as I can, and to see whether the "Mormon"

Church is responsible or not for that terrible deed; whether Brigham Young was or was not an accessory before the fact, or an accessory after the fact; and whether the charge that has been made against the "Mormon" people has any foundation in fact. I hope I shall have the assistance in doing this of the faith of my brethren and sisters, that I may have the Spirit of the Lord to rest upon me to quicken my mind, to give me grasp of thought, so that I may be able to bring forward clearly those evidences which I have been able to collect, and put them before the people in an intelligent shape so that all can understand them.

In the summer of 1857, a company of emigrants, as stated by some, composed of two parties, one from Missouri and the other from Arkansas, came into Salt Lake City. They were on their way to California. After staying here a short time, they were advised to take the northern route to California by way of Bear River. There were two routes by which the stream of emigration flowed to the west from this point. One was northward, and the other south and westward. They were advised by Elder Charles C. Rich to go by the northern route. They went as far as Bear River, but returned and concluded to take the southern route. On their way south they became very impertinent and abusive. At that time news had been received here of the approach of Buchanan's army, supposed to be coming here to destroy the

Latter-day Saints, to endeavor to break up "Mormonism," and to execute the atrocious threats which had been made by the soldiery in their camps on the plains, news of which had been brought here by runners.

These emigrants boasted to the people as they passed through the settlements that they were going to California, where they intended to get up a company and return and attack our people in the south when the army arrived in Salt Lake City. It is related that on the way, when going through small settlements—it was a large company, 120 to 150 persons, differently estimated—they would rob hen-roosts, and passing through the streets would flip off the heads of chickens with their whip-thongs. At one place, it is related, they poisoned the springs, so that the people who partook of the water died in consequence thereof. Still further, it is said that they poisoned beef and gave it to the Indians, and several Indians died from its effects, and at another place they caught an Indian, tied him up to a wagon wheel and whipped him severely. These are the stories which were told concerning these emigrants; whether they are true or false I am unable to say, but these were the stories told concerning them, and the people believed them. The Indians became very much enraged, and as this company traveled further and further south the rage of the Indians increased. On the way they met Jacob Hamblin

and asked him—as a resident of this Territory, a
man well acquainted with the country, who had
been among the Indians a great deal—which was
the best place to camp in a certain region, and he
told them the Mountain Meadows, at the north part
of which he had a ranch. They went on and
camped at the Mountain Meadows. But, as I told
you, all the way down they were committing these
depredations, by which not only were the settlers
very much aggrieved, but the Indians were aroused
to the greatest indignation and fury. When they
arrived at Mountain Meadows they were attacked
by Indians, but they entrenched themselves; they
threw up earthworks to the level of the hubs of
their wagon wheels, and prepared to defend themselves as in a state of siege. According to the evidence presented, it appears that John D. Lee was
at that time a member of the Church—not a
Bishop, by the way, I understand he never was a
Bishop, but was a member of the Church and
looked after the interests of a great number of
Indians in that part of the country as Indian farmer.
It is stated that John D. Lee led the first attack of
the Indians against those emigrants. About this
time a council was held at Cedar City, at which
were present Isaac C. Haight, Philip Klingensmith,
who was the acting Bishop, a man by the name of
Laban Morill, and some others. These persons at
this council took into consideration the depredations
which had been made by this party of emigrants.

You must understand that the people were very much excited at this time. The news of the coming of the army had reached different parts of the Territory, and a plan had been prepared, if they should come into the Territory, to burn down our houses, to destroy our property and leave the Territory a desert, a barren waste; for the people to flee to the mountains and leave nothing as a prey to their enemies. The people were getting ready for this emergency. You must remember also that the people living here in that early period had been driven from different parts of the United States, time and time again, for their religion; they had suffered untold hardships, privations and persecutions, and now the prospects were that an army was coming in upon them to drive them out again, or pull them up, root and branch, and destroy them. Of course there was a great deal of excitement at the time, and this body of emigrants having made those threats, cursing Brigham Young, declaring that "old Joe Smith ought to have been killed before he was," some of them declaring that they had taken part in his assassination, naturally aroused the anger of the people. Well, this council was held in Cedar City to determine what was best to be done, whether or not to intercept them and prevent the emigrants from going further south. Some person present on that occasion advocated their interception and destruction. Laban Morill and some others were of a different mind, stating that the proper

thing to do was to send a messenger to Governor
Young to find out what his advice was concerning
this matter, and to desist from doing anything of a
hostile nature until word was received from Governor
Young.  A messenger was despatched on the 7th
day of September, 1857.  His name was James
Haslam.  He came to Salt Lake City, saw President Young, delivered his message and a letter
from Isaac C. Haight, and received a despatch from
President Young to take back, and he was told to
"spare no horse-flesh"—to go "with all speed" and
deliver the despatch as quickly as possible.  That
despatch was delivered to Isaac C. Haight at Cedar
City on the following Sunday, which, according to
the dates that I have traced up, must have been on
the 13th day of September.  Isaac C. Haight's
answer was, "It is too late."  It appears that a
number of men had been called by Philip Klingensmith, the acting Bishop, and John M. Higbee, who
claimed to be acting under orders of Isaac C.
Haight and John D. Lee, to go to the Mountain
Meadows.  According to the testimony delivered at
the trials, to which I will refer presently, most of
these men had not the least idea that they were going to Mountain Meadows to perform any deed of
blood or to commit anything wrong.  They expected to be gone two or three days.  Some of the
emigrants had been killed by the Indians and they
expected they were going to help bury the dead.
When they arrived there, according to the testi-

mony given at the trial of John D. Lee, a man was
sent down into the camp of the emigrants with a
white flag, or a flag of truce.   Afterwards John D.
Lee went down and had some conversation with
the emigrants, and they were induced to give up
their arms, which were placed in wagons and they v
were all drawn out of the camp.   When they had
passed a considerable distance away, the Indians,
and it is said some of the whites, fired upon the emigrants and they were all butchered, men and women, and none were saved but about seventeen
small children, the oldest seven years of age.   It is
related that John D. Lee assisted in the slaughter-
ing of the wounded emigrants who were in the
wagons; those who were able to walk, marching
without arms, were set upon by the Indians, and, as
stated, some white men fired among them.   But it
appears that John D. Lee assisted in the killing of
the wounded persons, so that all the men, and the
women, and the older children were slain;   there
were none left but the seventeen little children, who
were taken and distributed around among the people,
until Forney, the Indian agent, some time afterwards came and gathered them up and took them
away.

Now, I have endeavored to tell you, as briefly
as possible, the dreadful story of the massacre.   It
was a horrible affair.   It makes one's blood run
cold to think of such a slaughter.   One hundred
and twenty persons—some say one hundred and

nineteen, but it is generally conceded to be about one hundred and twenty—inhumanly butchered. They were murdered. No one can palliate the crime. I would not attempt to do so. No circumstances that existed at that time could, in my mind, palliate that dreadful deed. And to think that any white person should be engaged in it is most horrible to my mind, most repugnant to my feelings, and I know it is repugnant to the feelings of my brethren and sisters, not only those present to-night, but the great body of people called Latter-day Saints wherever they may be.

Now, this horrible crime is laid at the door of the Church because certain individuals, who were then members of the Church, were engaged in this horrible massacre. This has always appeared to me to be very unjust. Why should the "Mormon" Church, the Church of Jesus Christ of Latter-day Saints, be held responsible for the crimes of a few of its members any more than other churches for the crimes of a few of their members? The Roman Catholic church for the deeds alleged to have been done by members of that church; the church of England, the Episcopal church, for the deeds done by men belonging to that church in early times, and some in later times? Why should the different denominations of the day, as religious denominations, as churches, be charged with the weaknesses, the corruptions and the diabolical deeds perpetrated, not only by members of these denominations, but by persons who officiate therein as ministers? Sensible people do not lay these crimes at the door of the denomination to which the individuals may belong, but charge them home to the individuals themselves. They are responsible for their acts, they alone should be charged with them, unless—unless what they do is taught by the church to which they belong, or is allowed by that church, or is in consonance with any of its doctrines. If it can be shown that the Church of Jesus Christ of Latter-day Saints teaches the people to commit murder; if it can be shown that the Church, as a religious body, ordered that massacre, or, after it occurred, condoned it, palliated it, or agreed that it was right, considered it was proper, then we may lay this crime upon the Church and claim that the Church is responsible for it. But if the Church teaches to the contrary, if the spirit of the whole people is against such deeds of blood, if it can be shown that in doing these dreadful things such white persons as were members of this Church who were guilty, actually violated the laws of the Church, then I say that the crime cannot be reasonably and consistently laid upon the Church as a body.

Mr. Stenhouse, in his work called "Rocky Mountain Saints," says that no sane person ever did lay the crime at the door of the Church. Now, I would like to refer you to a few of the charges that have been made concerning this crime, laying it upon the Church and people, and particularly upon Brig-

ham Young; because if it is true that the charge
has not been made against the Church, then there
is no need for me to make any rebuttal; but if the
charge is made that the "Mormon" Church is
responsible for this crime, then I am justified and it
is my duty to-night to bring forth evidence showing
that the "Mormon" Church had nothing to do with it.

On the 7th of February, 1863, John Cradlebaugh, of Nevada, who was once one of the associate justices of the Supreme Court of Utah Territory
made a speech in Congress, and I will quote from
page 17 of the pamphlet published with the full
text of his speech and references:

"I shall publish a portion as an appendix to
these remarks that you may see that I am justified
in charging that the Mormons are guilty, aye, that
the Mormon Church is guilty, of the crimes of murder and robbery as taught in their books of faith."

You see, according to the Hon. John Cradlebaugh, the "Mormon" Church is charged with this
crime, and charged in the Congress of the United
States, in a speech published to the country.

There was a pamphlet prepared in this city
called "The Handbook of Mormonism"—perhaps
you have heard of it before, it is a most abomin-
able book—I will make a short quotation from it,
page 67:

"It is said to be a truth that Brigham Young
sent letters south authorizing, if not commanding,
that the train should be destroyed."

I will now refer you to a speech made by Mr.

W. McGrorty in the case of McGrorty *versus*
Hooper. You will remember that Mr. McGrorty,
in 1868, contested the seat of Hon. W. H. Hooper,
our Delegate in Congress, and made an attack
upon the "Mormons." He received 105 votes
against Mr. Hooper's 15,068. Let me say here
that nearly all the anti-Mormon stories that have
been since dished up in various shapes and forms
have been taken from Mr. McGrorty's speech in
Congress; from that speech Cradlebaugh made up
most of his story, and it has been retold over and
over again from that time to the present. I will
read from page 40 of the pamphlet containing Mr.
McGrorty's speech. Mr. McGrorty thought that
the Territory ought at once to be put under martial law, and he said:

"This may be the only practicable way in
which even partial punishment can be meted out to
these latter-day devils. But how inadequate would
be the punishment of a few even by death for this
crime which nearly the whole Mormon population
from Brigham Young down, were more or less instrumental in perpetrating."

I have a work here which was published by
Mr. Bishop, who defended John D. Lee at both of
his trials. I will make a quotation from this book,
page 19. He says:

"I claim that Brigham Young is the real criminal, and that John D. Lee was an instrument in
his hands. That Brigham Young used John D.
Lee as the assassin uses the dagger, to strike down

...suspecting victim; and as the assassin throws
... the dagger, to avoid its bloody blade leading
... detection, so Brigham Young used John D.
... to do his horrid work; and when discovery
... ...nes unavoidable, he hurls Lee from him, cuts
... away from the Church, and casts him far out
... the whirlpool of destruction.  The assassin has
... ...rther use for his weapon.  I also claim that if
...ious fanaticism can clear a man from crime
... ... D. Lee was guiltless, for he was one of
... ...ost intensely fanatical Mormons that infested
... in 1857.  But I do not claim that the fact of
... ...eing a fanatic and blinded believer of Brig-
... Young's so-called revelations excused him—
... ... om it.  In place of excusing him it added to
... ime.  Such insanity as that which fanaticism
... ...ls can only, and should only, be treated by the
... ...tioner.  And there are many thousands in
... who are afflicted with the disease that calls
... ...he radical treatment that was administered to
... ...

will read to you now some opinions of the
... appended to a report of the first Lee trial, in
... ...phlet emanating from the *Tribune* office in
... ty.  These are culled from different news-
... ...

From the Leavenworth (Kansas) *Commercial:*

"The Mormons are making a desperate effort
... ...ar Brigham Young of the Mountain Meadows
... ...acre, but they will never succeed in convinc-
... ...he world that the old sinner was not guilty of
... ...ipation in the preliminaries to the inhuman
... ...e, nor that the work of butchery was not

W. McGrorty in the case of McGrorty *vc*
Hooper. You will remember that Mr. McGro
in 1868, contested the seat of Hon. W. H. Hoo
our Delegate in Congress, and made an at
upon the "Mormons." He received 105 v
against Mr. Hooper's 15,068. Let me say
that nearly all the anti-Mormon stories that I
been since dished up in various shapes and fo
have been taken from Mr. McGrorty's speec
Congress; from that speech Cradlebaugh mad
most of his story, and it has been retold over
over again from that time to the present. I
read from page 40 of the pamphlet containing
McGrorty's speech. Mr. McGrorty thought
the Territory ought at once to be put under r
tial law, and he said:

"This may be the only practicable wa
which even partial punishment can be meted ou
these latter-day devils. But how inadequate w
be the punishment of a few even by death for thi
crime which nearly the whole Mormon popula
from Brigham Young down, were more or les
strumental in perpetrating."

I have a work here which was publishec
Mr. Bishop, who defended John D. Lee at bot
his trials. I will make a quotation from this b
page 19. He says:

"I claim that Brigham Young is the real c
inal, and that John D. Lee was an instrumei
his hands. That Brigham Young used John
Lee as the assassin uses the dagger, to strike d

his unsuspecting victim; and as the assassin throws away the dagger, to avoid its bloody blade leading to his detection, so Brigham Young used John D. Lee to do his horrid work; and when discovery becomes unavoidable, he hurls Lee from him, cuts him away from the Church, and casts him far out into the whirlpool of destruction. The assassin has no further use for his weapon. I also claim that if religious fanaticism can clear a man from crime John D. Lee was guiltless, for he was one of the most intensely fanatical Mormons that infested Utah in 1857. But I do not claim that the fact of his being a fanatic and blinded believer of Brigham Young's so-called revelations excused him— far from it. In place of excusing him it added to his crime. Such insanity as that which fanaticism breeds can only, and should only, be treated by the executioner. And there are many thousands in Utah who are afflicted with the disease that calls for the radical treatment that was administered to Lee."

I will read to you now some opinions of the press appended to a report of the first Lee trial, in a pamphlet emanating from the *Tribune* office in this city. These are culled from different newspapers.

From the Leavenworth (Kansas) *Commercial:*

"The Mormons are making a desperate effort to clear Brigham Young of the Mountain Meadows massacre, but they will never succeed in convincing the world that the old sinner was not guilty of participation in the preliminaries to the inhuman outrage, nor that the work of butchery was not perpetrated with his sanction, if not by his positive command."

From the Fort Wayne (Indiana) *Journal:*

"The evidence in the trial of the Mormon leader, John D. Lee, charged with participating in the Mountain Meadows massacre in 1857, clearly points to the unmistakable guilt of many distinguished Mormons, including Brigham Young, Hooper, the ex-Congressman, and others."

From the Leavenworth *Times:*

"It would be a waste of time and money to attempt to bring the Mountain Meadows assassins to justice. They have too strong a following. The Church of the Latter-day Saints is bound to stand by them. To convict Lee would be to convict the Church and strike a fatal blow at its foundation."

From the Chicago *Inter-Ocean:*

"The investigation, however, has resulted in fixing an indelible stain on the Mormon Church and settling the responsibility for an act of barbarism which was even regarded as a reproach by the lawless savages of the west, who are supposed to know no shame nor pity, but who protested against the infamy of such a deed."

From the Idaho (Montana) *Statesman:*

"This circumstance is so enormous and crime so heinous, and the evidence so plain, that it must and will be laid at the door of the Church with Brigham Young as its leader, and be remembered by every man, woman and child wherever the name of Mormon is mentioned."

From the Hartford (Connecticut) *Times:*

"That much at any rate has been shown by

Lee's trial, and the guilt of mercilessly sacrificing unarmed men, women and children to religious fanaticism are justly chargeable against the Mormon Church. It now remains to be seen whether American justice will much longer allow the existence of such a bloodthirsty and barbarous organization in the country. The good repute of our institutions is at stake in permitting Mormonism a place in the land."

I think it will not be denied now that the charge has been made that the "Mormon" Church is responsible for the massacre at Mountain Meadows. Now, I claim that the Church is not responsible, and to begin my defense of the Church, I will read to you from the 42nd section of the Book of Doctrine and Covenants. This is a revelation given through the Prophet Joseph Smith to the Church, February 9th, 1831, to be found on page 170 of the Book of Doctrine and Covenants, new edition:

"And now behold I speak unto the Church. Thou shalt not kill; and he that kills shall not have forgiveness in this world, nor in the world to come.

"And again I say, thou shalt not kill; but he that killeth shall die."

I will now read to you from page 176, the same revelation:

"And it shall come to pass that if any persons among you shall kill, they shall be delivered up and dealt with according to the laws of the land; for remember that he hath no forgiveness, and it shall be proven according to the laws of the land."

That is received by Latter-day Saints in all the

world as a revelation from God, and as a commandment, a standing commandment to this Church
—that is, "Thou shalt not kill, and he that killeth
shall not have forgiveness in this world nor in the
world to come." In the revelation on celestial
marriage it is set forth that when persons have
entered into certain covenants before God of a
sacred character, and partaken of the Holy Ghost,
and received the higher ordinances of the Church,
if they commit murder—shed "innocent blood," it
will be impossible for them to be forgiven either
in this world or in the world to come; it will be
impossible for them to regain their salvation; their
exaltation is gone.  Now, then, that being the doctrine of the Church, how could the Church of
Jesus Christ of Latter-day Saints authorize the
wholesale destruction of men, women and children?
It could not be.  Such an act would be contrary to
the doctrines of the Church, contrary to the revelations believed by its members to be the word of
God, believed by the people to be binding upon
them, their faith being that if they commit such
crimes they cannot be forgiven either in this world
or in the world to come.

I will refer you now to a book published by
an anti-Mormon named Beadle—perhaps you have
heard of Mr. Beadle before.  He is the author of a
good many blood-curdling stories, and some of
them are told in this book.  But I am not going to
read them to-night, I will merely read to you

Beadle's testimony in regard to this point. This is the evidence of an enemy:

"Some months passed away before it was whispered in the northern district that white men were concerned in this affair; and to the credit of the Mormon people be it said, a great horror spread among them at the report.

"John D. Lee still resides in Harmony (1870) no longer a Bishop [he never was a Bishop] and one can scarcely restrain a feeling of satisfaction at knowing that his life is one of misery. He is shunned and hated even by his Mormon neighbors; he seldom ventures beyond the square upon which he lives; his mind is distracted by an unceasing dread of vengeance and his intellect is disordered." (*Beadle's Mysteries of Mormonism, page 185.*)

Now, I ask, how could "a great horror" spread among the people if the people were accessories to this deed? If it was part of the doctrine of their Church, if they were willing and anxious for this massacre, how could a great horror spread among them at the report of it? And why should Lee be shunned by his neighbors if this was a deed that the Church ordered or approved, or that its members condoned or palliated?

I will now read to you a few quotations from Stenhouse's "Rocky Mountain Saints." This work, as you are well aware, was published against the "Mormons." Stenhouse was a member of the Church and afterwards apostatized and wrote a book against the Church. On page 459 he says:

"The Mormon newspapers very properly declaim against 'the people' of Utah being branded as murderers, because murders have been committed within their Territory, and further they protest against the great crimes being charged to Brigham Young."

That shows that the "Mormon" people themselves did not approve of that crime, or of any other crimes of a similar character.

I will next read from page 460 of the same work:

"When the news of that deed was heard, the people north were terror-stricken, and shuddered with horror at the thought of the barbarous crime, and the recital of the bloody work is harrowing to them to-day.

"The Mormon people of Utah are not the off-spring of a barbarous race, neither were they raised and nurtured in uncivilized nations. Apart from the spitefulness of religious controversy— which, by the by, is nothing peculiar to them—a kinder and more simple-hearted people is not upon the face of the earth. Had the Mountain Meadows massacre occurred in any of the neighboring Territories, and that crime was clearly the work of white people, the Mormons would have despised them, hated them, and in all probability would have refused all intercourse with them."

And on the same page appears the following:

"That Brigham Young is by his natural instincts a bad man, or that his apostles and his bishops are men of blood, is not true. Here and there among them a malicious man is met with, but apart from religion, the ruling men in Utah would be considered good citizens in, any community."

That is the testimony of Mr. Stenhouse in a book written against the Church.

I have a little work here published by Jacob Hamblin, the man whose ranch was at Mountain Meadows, but who was not at home when the massacre took place; he was here in Salt Lake City. He met the emigrants on his way here as they were going south. I will read you from page 46 of his book:

"This deplorable affair caused a sensation of horror and deep regret throughout the entire community, by whom it was unqualifiedly condemned.

"In Cove Creek Valley we met others from the south, who told us that the Indians were gathering to attack another company of emigrants. I procured a horse, left the wagons, and rode on day and night. At Cedar City I found Brothers Samuel Knight and Dudley Leavitt.

"As I was weary with hard riding and want of sleep, I hurried them on after the emigrants, while I traveled more slowly. I instructed these men to make every possible effort to save the company and their effects, and to save their lives at all hazards.

"They overtook the company 156 miles from Cedar City, on Muddy Creek, in the heart of the Indian country. They found a large body of excited Indians preparing to attack and destroy them.

"Finding it altogether impossible to control the Indians, they compromised the matter. The Indians agreed to take only the loose stock of the company, and not meddle with the teams and wagons, and not make any efforts to take their lives.

"The Indians took the loose stock, amounting to 480 head, on the fifty-mile desert beyond the Muddy.

"The brethren remained with the company, determined to assist in its defense, should the Indians attempt anything more than they had agreed."

This was the company that followed immediately behind the company that was killed, according to Jacob Hamblin.

I need not tell the Latter-day Saints that the deed was condemned. It was a long time before any news of this massacre reached the north. It should be understood that at that time the southern settlements were few and far between, and the country was sparsely settled. The place where the massacre took place was 350 miles or thereabouts south and west of Salt Lake City. There were no railroads in the country at that time ; there were no telegraphs here at that time ; and the United States mails had been stopped. Uncle Sam had sent out an army—or James Buchanan, representing the government, had sent it out, in hostility to the "Mormons," and the mails were suspended. We had no regular mail connection between these settlements, no telegraphs, no telephones, no railroads, no swift method of communication, and it was a long time before the bad tidings reached the north, and when it did it was supposed that the crime had been per-

petrated by the Indians. It was known very well
that the feeling of the Indians at that time was
hostile towards the whites, and it was a common
expression among them that they wanted to fight
the "Mericats," as they called them. It was thought,
therefore, when the word came, that the crime had
been committed by the Indians, and then a feeling
of horror pervaded the entire community, and it
was deplored and condemned in toto.

I have shown in these few references I have
made that this dreadful crime cannot be laid to the
door of the people, and it takes the body of the
"Mormon" people to make the Church. The
"Mormon" Church is not composed simply of the
First Presidency. It was not composed at that time
of Brigham Young and his Counselors. They
merely formed one quorum in the Church. It was
not composed of the First Presidency and the
quorum of the Twelve Apostles. It took the
whole body of the Church to make the Church.
We are told in the Book of Doctrine and Covenants that "all things in the Church shall be done by
common consent," and nothing can be called an act
of the Church except that which the Church votes
for or consents to. Even if it could be proved that
Brigham Young, or George A. Smith, or other
leading men of the Church were in any way compromised in that terrible affair, it would not prove
that the "Mormon" Church was guilty. The
Church is not responsible for the acts of Brigham

Young, nor for the acts of any individual. Each person is responsible before God for his own acts. He is responsible to the Church when he violates the laws of the Church. Every man in the Church, from the highest authority down to the lowest, is amenable to the Church courts when he falls into transgression ; but the transgression must be proved and established by the mouths of two or three witnesses according to the Church laws; and if a member of the Church transgresses, if any man holding the Priesthood transgresses, if any man holding any authority whatever transgresses the laws of God and the laws of the Church, he is amenable to the courts of the Church. Provision is made for the case of every individual, from the First Presidency down. If he does anything that is unrighteous he can be judged by the Council which is set apart for that purpose. So I say that any movement that is made, to be rightly chargeable to the Church, must be endorsed by the Church as a body, must be done by common consent of the Church. The Church of Jesus Christ of Latter-day Saints never preached the doctrine that it was right to kill men, women and children, as those emigrants were killed at Mountain Meadows. The Church never endorsed that deed, never approved of it. The crime caused a thrill of horror to run through the entire community.

I think I need not dwell any further on the accusation in regard to the body of the Church.

The principal charges that are made as to individuals center right against President Brigham Young and Apostle George A. Smith, who was afterwards the first Counselor of President Young. Brother George A. Smith has been charged with going before the emigrants down south and arousing the people against them. He has been also charged with counseling the people not to sell to this company of emigrants any grain, or flour, or provisions of any kind. He has been charged with stirring up a feeling of hostility among the people against this particular company, and it is claimed that the effects of his teachings culminated in the massacre.

I will then first take up the case of George A. Smith and see how far he was implicated in this matter. I will read to you the affidavit made by George A. Smith himself, which was presented at the Lee trial, and I will take it from this lovely (?) book of Mr. Bishop's, on page 307. I prefer, where I possibly can, to get my evidence from the . works of persons who are bitterly opposed to us :

TERRITORY OF UTAH, } ss.:
    Beaver County. }

In the Second Judicial District Court of the Territory of Utah. The people, etc.. vs. John D. Lee, William H. Dame, Isaac C. Haight, et al., Salt Lake Co. Indictment for murder, committed September 16th, 1857.

George A. Smith, having been first duly sworn, deposes and says that he is aged 58 years. That he is now and has been for several months suffering from a severe and dangerous illness of the head and lungs, and that to attend the court at Beaver, in the present condition of his health, would in all probability end his life.

Deponent further saith, that he never, in the year 1857, at Parowan or elsewhere, attended a council where Wm. H. Dame, Isaac C. Haight or others were present to discuss any measures for attacking, or in any manner injuring, an emigrant train from Arkansas or any other place, which is alleged to have been destroyed at Mountain Meadows in September, 1857.

Deponent further saith, that he never heard or knew anything of a train of emigrants, which he learned afterwards by rumor was from Arkansas, until he met said train at Corn Creek on his way north to Salt Lake City, on or about the 25th day of August, 1857.

Deponent further saith, that he encamped with Jacob Hamblin, Philo T. Farnsworth, Silas S. Smith and Elijah Hopps, and there for the first time he learned of the existence of said emigrant .train, and their intended journey to California.

Deponent further saith, that having been absent from the Territory for a year previous, he returned in the Summer of 1857 and went south to visit his family at Parowan, and to look after some property he had there, and also visit his friends, and for no other purpose, and that on leaving Salt Lake City he had no knowledge whatsoever of the existence of said emigrant train, nor did he acquire any until as before stated.

Deponent further saith, that as an Elder in the Church of Jesus Christ of Latter-day Saints he preached several times on his way south, and also on his return, and tried to impress upon the minds of the people the necessity of great care as to their grain crops, as all crops had been short for several years previous to 1857, and many of the people were reduced to actual want and were suffering for the necessaries of life.

Deponent further saith, that he advised the people to furnish all emigrant companies passing through the Territory with what they might actually need for breadstuff, for the support of themselves and families while passing through the Territory, and also advised the people not to feed their grains to their own stock, nor to sell to the emigrants for that purpose.

Deponent further saith, that he never heard or knew of any attack upon said emigrant train until some time after his return to Salt Lake City, and that while near Fort Bridger he heard for the first time that the Indians had massacred an emigrant company at Mountain Meadows.

Deponent further saith, that he never at any time, either before or after that massacre, was accessory thereto, that he never directly or indirectly aided, abetted or assisted in its perpetration, or had any knowledge thereof except by hearsay; that he never knew anything of the distribution of the property taken there, except by hearsay as aforesaid.

Deponent further saith, that all charges and statements as pertaining to him contrary to the above are false and untrue.

(Signed)                GEO. A. SMITH.

Subscribed and sworn to before me this 30th day of July, A. D. 1875.

(Signed)  WM. CLAYTON, Notary Public.

I will now read to you the testimony given at
the first Lee trial in regard to this matter on pages
33 and 34 of *Tribune* report. This testimony was
given under oath by Jesse N. Smith, with whom
many of you are acquainted—a man of honor, a
man of veracity, a man of integrity, well known in
this community, whose word is as good as his bond.
I will not read you the whole of the testimony, but
just that part pertaining to George A. Smith:

"I lived in Parowan in 1857, came to Utah ten
years previously. Knew Wm. H. Dame, saw the
emigrant train at the town above-named; sold them
flour and salt, had flour to spare and asked if they
wanted more; they wanted vegetables, but witness
had none to spare. Saw George A. Smith in Parowan Aug. 8th; he came in from the north, went
down among the settlements, witness accompany-
ing him. A meeeting was held in every settlement.
Witness attended them all. He [George A. Smith]
deprecated selling grain and breadstuffs to feed to
horses and mules. Never heard him in his public
addresses allude to this train."

I will now read from the testimony of Silas S.
Smith, a man that is as well known and as highly
respected as Jesse N. Smith, and was, for many
years in this community, a member of the Legis-
lative Assembly:

"Know George A. Smith; saw him in August
of 1857 at Parowan and traveled with him through
the southern settlements, returning with him to
Cedar Springs, Millard County. George A. Smith,
in his speeches, referred to the necessity of saving

grain and not feeding it to horses or stock; he dis-
approved of selling it for any such use. Heard
nothing said to discourage the sale of provisions to
emigrant trains for food. Witness camped at Corn
Creek and found the Arkansas train in camp there
on arrival. Some of them came over to witness'
fire and simply made inquiries. Nothing special was
said. One of the party asked if the Indians would
be likely to eat the flesh of an ox that lay dead near
camp. Some said that they probably would.

"Two days after, came to Beaver, passing the
emigrants at Indian Creek, six or seven miles from
here. Took supper with the emigrants there.
Four days after this the emigrants passed through
the town where witness lives, thirty miles south,
and camped there. Spoke to some of the party;
saw the leader; heard him called Mr. Fancher.
Duke's party followed several days after. They
got into trouble with the Indians near Beaver and
witness was sent over with ten men by Col. Dame,
who called at his house to request witness to go to
the relief of the emigrants. Reached Beaver at
night, and in the morning found the train corraled
and a rifle pit dug for their protection. Sent a
runner, who brought in the chief, and witness pla-
cated the wrath of the red men by a liberal distribution of beef. The Indians claimed that some of
their braves had been shot by men belonging to the
train, and they must wash out the offense in blood.
Witness understood that his intervention had settled the difficulty. Had no further connection with
the emigrant trains.

"Traveled with George A. Smith from Parowan to Santa Clara, 150 miles. Held five or six
meetings on the way. George A. Smith invited

witness to accompany him. The object of his visit was to preach to the people to lay up grain for their future support. Col. Johnston's army was then approaching Utah. Heard nothing said against allowing emigrant trains to pass through the country. * * George A. Smith did not tell witness why he left Salt Lake alone to travel through the Territory. His only mission, so far as witness knows, was to counsel the people to save their grain and not feed it to stock."

It is well known by those who were residing in Utah at that time—I was not here—that this was the advice given all over the Territory. The people were counseled not to feed grain to their stock, nor to sell their grain to emigrants for their animals, but to save it for breadstuff, because of the coming of the army. These facts appeared in the *Journal of Discourses*, which I had the privilege of reading in a distant land at that time, and these instructions were given to the whole people, not only in the south, but in the north, and to the whole community. George A. Smith, when traveling to Parowan, preached this to the people in every settlement where he stayed, and when he returned to Salt Lake City he reported in public, in the Tabernacle, and his discourse was published in the *Journal of Discourses*, previously appearing in the *Deseret News*—that he had counseled the people not to waste their grain nor feed it to their own stock, or sell it for that purpose to the emigrants. George A. Smith has been charged with going out in advance of this company, prejudicing the minds of the people against the emigrants and counseling the people not to sell them provisions of any kind. The affidavit of George A. Smith and the evidence of the two Smiths, that I have just read to you, show to the contrary. There is no proof whatever, no reliable evidence of any description, that Geo. A. Smith did anything of the kind imputed to him. We all know that George A. Smith was not a man of vengeance nor a man of blood. I do not think I need spend much more time in regard to his case, because, after all, the chief person whom responsibility for the massacre was desired to be saddled was President Brigham Young.

The question now is whether President Young was responsible for that awful crime committed at Mountain Meadows. President Young must have been an accessory before the fact, or an accessory after the fact, if he was in any way chargeable with that dreadful deed. I will first examine the evidence to see whether he was an accessory before the fact; whether he advised this crime; whether such of the people who were guilty were influenced by any instructions or message he had sent to them.

Those of you who are acquainted with the facts in relation to the coming of the army from the east against the people here, are well aware that it was a time of great excitement. The army was encamped out east, and our brethren were in Echo Canyon preparing their defenses. Some of them

who were out on the plains taking measures to
arrest the progress of the army, received instructions from President Young.  Of what nature were
they?  Everybody acquainted with the facts knows
that the instructions from President Young were
that they might arrest the progress of the army,
burn the grass, stampede their animals and destroy
their trains; but they were not to shed a drop of
blood.  These instructions were given over and
over again to those in charge.  I have read copies
of those despatches in a letter book, signed by
Brigham Young.  I have seen these instructions
with my own eyes.  I have heard the brethren who
were engaged in that defense bear testimony to
this.  The instructions that were given over and
over again were that they were not to shed a drop
of blood unless actually compelled to do so in self-
defense.  And, mind you, this was at the very time
that President Young is said to have given instructions to destroy this company of emigrants!

I have to refer you to a good many documents
and papers, for I do not want you to rely on my
testimony, but I want to bring forward as clear evidence and proof as I have been able to collect in
regard to this matter.  I want to read to you now
a statement made by General Daniel H. Wells,
which was published in the *New York Herald* of
May 6, 1877, being a part of an interview between
the representative of the *New York Herald* and
President Young;  the former having been sent

here especially to interview the latter in regard to this matter:

"Everybody remembers how the people behaved when ordered out by President Young to prevent Johnston from entering the Territory at what might have seemed to another man a most dismal moment of his career.  The president issued an order which, while it obliged us to burn forage in advance, set fire to the grass at night, carry off animals and do various other things to hold back the enemy, absolutely forbade a single man to shed a drop of blood.

"I remember when a young officer was captured by one of your troops a wallet found on him contained an order to him signed by me, on the back of which was the usual inscription, 'Shed no blood.'  That order was taken first to Johnston, and was afterwards taken to Washington and brought out in the famous debate of the next session."

You see, this man that was captured had the document upon his person giving him instructions, and the positive command was that he was to "shed no blood."

I will now read to you an extract from a letter published by a company of teamsters who passed through this country at the time of the Utah expedition.  It was published on the 5th of June, 1858, in the *Southern Vineyard,* a paper printed in Los Angeles.  It shows the disposition of the people at that time, and the orders of the authorities:

"On the 16th we arrived at a Mormon station, at the mouth of Echo Canyon, in a famished condi-

tion. On representing our distressed circumstances
our wants were *promptly and gratuitously supplied.*
Here we were furnished with an escort to the city,
where we met with Lieut. Gen. D. H. Wells, of the
Utah militia, who issued instructions regarding our
safety throughout the settlements, accompanied
with a relieved escort at each station. We recruit-
ed ourselves at Beaver City, and it was deemed
advisable to fit up for the journey to California.
We would be exceedingly ungrateful in omitting an
expression of our sincere thanks and deep indebt-
edness to our Mormon friends of Utah, and the
mail carriers, for the disinterested kindness evinced
toward us in ministering to our wants, and for the
aid extended to us in our journey to California,
without which we could never have reached our
destination, but have perished in the desert, or been
killed by merciless savages."

This very company of teamsters the "Mormons" were accused of murdering, while the facts
were they owed their lives to "Mormon" generos-
ity. Their testimony shows the disposition of the
people here at that time and the orders of the
President to Gen. D. H. Wells.

I will now read to you the instructions of President Young to Col. Dame, at Parowan, which you
will find in the beautiful (?) book of Mr. Bishop's,
page 316. I do not think I will take up the time
in reading the whole of this circular. I will, however, read the latter part of it. It is published in
full in this and other books. It is dated, "Great
Salt Lake City, September 14, 1857"—just about
the time of the massacre. I will give you the exact

date of that occurrence presently. It has been dis-
puted as to the actual date when the massacre took
place, the dates varying from the 10th to the 16th
of September; but I think I can give you the exact
date:

"Herewith you will receive the Governor's
proclamation declaring martial law.

"You will probably not be called out this Fall,
but are requested to continue to make ready for a
big fight another year."

At the close of the circular. which was not
only sent to this gentleman, Col. Dame, but all over
the Territory, it says:

"And what we said in regard to saving the
grain and provisions we say again, let there be no
waste. Save life always when it is possible. We
do not wish to shed a drop of blood if it can be
avoided."

Now, here is Brigham Young sending a circular to all the chief men of the militia throughout
the Territory, declaring that he does not want a
drop of blood shed if it can be avoided. They
were to save, not destroy, life. And yet we are
expected to believe that right at that time, or a day
or two previously, President Young sent down word
to our brethren in the same neighborhood to kill off
the emigrants! The story does not hold very well
together in the light of this circular, from which I
have just read.

I will now refer again to Mr. Stenhouse's book,
"Rocky Mountain Saints." You must excuse me

if I take up a good deal of time in reading extracts. My object is to establish the facts, as far as possible, from the testimony of persons not connected with us. I read from Stenhouse's book, page 369:

"The Prophet had given orders that no blood was to be shed under any temptation or provocation, save only in the extremity of self-defense."

That is the testimony of T. B. H. Stenhouse, an enemy. I will refer you again to the same book, page 385. It is an extract from an address by President Young:

"Should I take a course to waste life? We are in duty bound to preserve life—to preserve ourselves on the earth—consequently *we must use policy* and follow in the counsel gived us, in order to preserve our lives."

This address was delivered at the time when the army was coming in. I have read this extract to show you that the policy of President Young was to preserve life, notwithstanding there was a hostile army right on our borders, coming for the express purpose of destroying the people, yet the policy of President Young was not to shed blood.

Next, I will read to you an extract from the Lee trial—remarks made by Mr. Sumner Howard, the U. S. prosecuting attorney at the second trial of John D. Lee:

"He proposed to prove that John D. Lee, without any authority from any council or officer, but in direct opposition to the feelings and wishes of the officers of the Mormon Church, had gone to the

Mountain Meadows, where the Indians were then encamped, accompanied only by a little Indian boy, and had assumed command of the Indians, whom he had induced, by promises of great booty, to attack these emigrants; that in his attack on the emigrants he was repulsed; that finding he could not get the emigrants out, he sent word to the various settlements of southern Utah for men to be sent to him, representing that the men were needed for various purposes, to some saying the Indians had attacked the emigrants and it was necessary to have men sent to draw off the Indians, to others that men were necessary to protect the emigrants, and still others that the emigrants were all killed, and that they were required to bury the dead; these men went in good faith to perform a humane act; that he had arranged with the Indians to bring the emigrants out from their corral, or fort, by means of a flag of truce; that by this act of perfidy he had induced the emigrants to give up their arms and place themselves under his protection, loading the arms and the wounded with the helpless children into two wagons, which he had ordered up for the purpose; that he then started the wagons ahead, following them himself, and the women following next, the men bringing up the rear in single file; that Lee, after having traveled from three quarters of a mile to a mile, gave the order to fire, and the slaughter commenced; that Lee shot one woman with his rifle, and brained another woman; then drawing his pistol, shot another, and seizing a man by the collar and drawing him out of a wagon, cut his throat; that he gathered up the property of the emigrants and took it to his own place, using and selling it for his own benefit and use. All these

charges against John D. Lee, he (District Attorney
Howard) proposed to prove to the jury by competent,
testimony, beyond reasonable doubt, or beyond any
doubt, and thought no appeal to the jury would be
required to induce them to give a verdict in accordance with the evidence."

I will now read to you a passage from Lee's
confession, or reported confession. John D. Lee
made a great many so-called "confessions" which
are rather contradictory. This confession is supposed to be the "only true and genuine one."
Whether it is or not I cannot say. My opinion is
from what I have read that John D. Lee furnished
particulars and data to Mr. Bishop, who worked
them up with some of his own notions and fabri-
cations into this book. I cite this work of an enemy
to show that President Young was not an accessory
before the fact. I read from Bishop's book, page
233:

"Major Higbee said 'Here are the orders' and
handed me a paper from Haight. It was in substance that it was the orders of Haight to decoy
the emigrants from their position and kill all of
them that could talk. This order was in writing.
Higbee handed it to me and I read it, and then drop-
ped it on the ground, saying 'I cannot do this.'
The substance of the orders were that the emigrants
should be decoyed from their stronghold and all
exterminated so that no one would be left to tell
the tale and then the authorities could say it was
done by the Indians."

You see this order did not come from Brigham

Young. If it was given at all it come from Haight.
We will now turn to page 245 of the same work:

"After the dead were searched the brethren
were called up and Higbee and Klingensmith, as
well as myself made speeches, and *ordered* the
people to keep the matter a secret from the entire
world. Not to tell their wives, or their most intimate
friends, and we pledged ourselves to keep everything relating to the affair a secret through life.
We also took the most binding oaths to stand by
each other, and to always insist that the massacre
was committed by Indians alone.  *  *  *

"Knowing that Dame and Haight had quarreled at Hamblin's that morning, I wanted to know
how they would act in sight of the dead, who lay
there as the result of their orders. I was greatly
interested to know what Dame had to say, so I
kept close to them, without appearing to be watch-
ing them. Col. Dame was silent for some time.
He looked all over the field and was quite pale and
looked uneasy and frightened. I thought then that
he was just finding out the difference between giving and executing orders for wholesale killing. He
spoke to Haight and said:

"'I must report this matter to the authorities.'
"'How will you report it?' said Haight.
"Dame said, 'I will report it just as it is.'
"'Yes, I suppose so, and implicate yourself
with the rest,' said Haight.
"'No,' said Dame, 'I will not implicate myself,
for I had nothing to do with it.'
"Haight then said, 'That will not do, for you
know a d—— sight better. You ordered it done.'

*    *    *    *    *    *    *

"Col. Dame was much excited. He choked up and would have gone away, but he knew Haight was a man of determination and would not stand any foolishness."

You see that there was a quarrel, according to John D. Lee, between Haight and Dame in regard to this matter right on the field near where the dead were lying. Dame disclaimed having anything whatever to do with the crime; but Haight, as I have read to you, tried to place the responsibility upon him. Dame declared he had had nothing to do with it, that he had given no orders concerning it, and threatened to report the details to the authorities of the Church. Haight immediately was afraid, and asked him what he was going to report. Now, then, if Brigham Young had given orders to have the emigrants massacred, why should Haight be in such a state of alarm at the declaration of Dame that he was going to report the matter to President Young? We are asked to believe that President Young ordered that massacre. Yet here we learn by the confession of John D. Lee, who states that he heard this quarrel between Haight and Dame, that Haight, who had given the order, wanted to lay the blame upon Dame, and that Haight was afraid to have the massacre reported to the authorities of the Church. Here is an account of some speeches made just after this (page 347):

"The speeches were first—thanks to God for

delivering our enemies into our hands; next, thanking the brethren for their zeal in God's cause; and then the necessity of always saying the Indians did it alone, and that the Mormons had nothing to do with it. The speeches, however, were in the shape of exhortation and commands to keep the whole matter secret from everyone but Brigham Young. It was voted unanimously that any man who should divulge the secret, or tell who was present, or do anything that would lead to a discovery of the truth, should suffer death.

"The brethren then all took a most solemn oath, binding themselves under the most dreadful and awful penalties, to keep the whole matter secret from every human being, as long as they should live. No man was to know the facts. The brethren were sworn not to talk of it among themselves, and each one swore to help kill all who proved to be traitors to the Church or people in this matter.

"It was then agreed that Brigham Young should be informed of the whole matter, by some one to be selected by the Church council, after the brethren had returned home."

Now, you see, there was an agreement that this matter should be reported to President Young, and yet we are asked to believe that President Young had ordered it. Dame and Haight quarreled over it. Haight feared that it would be reported just as it was, and the whole body of men were sworn to keep it entirely secret. John D. Lee was selected to go to President Young and make a report. We will find out presently what kind of a report Lee made. John D. Lee says, page 250:

"The first time I heard that a messenger had been sent to Brigham Young for instructions as to what should be done with the emigrants, was three or four days after I had returned home from the Meadows. Then I heard of it from Isaac C. Haight, when he came to my house and had a talk with me. He said:

"'We are in a muddle. Haslam has returned from Salt Lake City, with orders from Brigham Young to let the emigrants pass in safety.'

"In this conversation Haight also said:

"'I sent an order to Higbee to save the emigrants, after I had sent the orders for killing them all, but for some reason the message did not reach him. I understand that the messengers did not go to the Meadows at all.'

"I at once saw that we were in a bad fix, and I asked Haight what was to be done. We talked the matter over again.

"Haight then told me that it was the orders of the council that I should go to Salt Lake City and lay the whole matter before Brigham Young. I asked him if he was not going to write a report of it to the governor, as he was the right man to do it, for he was in command of the militia in that section of the country, and next to Dame in command of the whole district. I told him that it was a matter which really belonged to the military department, and should be so reported.

"He refused to write a report, saying:

"'You can report it better than I could write it. You are like a member of Brigham's family, and can talk to him privately and confidentially. I want you to take all of it on yourself that you can, and not expose any more of the brethren than you find absolutely necessary."

Now, here are the instructions of Haight to John D. Lee. Here is Haight trying to cover up from President Young the crime which we are asked to believe President Young had ordered. The message had come saying that the emigrants were to be allowed to pass. But Haight wanted John D. Lee to go to Salt Lake City and fix it up; make a report to the President so as to allay his feelings. John D. Lee subsequently agreed to do this.

Now I will cite to you the testimony of Laban Morrill in regard to the dispatch from President Young to Haight. I will refer again to Bishop's book, page 320. An objection was made on the part of the defense at the second Lee trial to the introduction of this testimony, but the objection was overruled:

"As I said, there appeared to be some confusion in that council. I inquired in a friendly way, what was up. I was told that there was an emigrant train that passed along down to near Mountain Meadows, and that they had made threats in regard to us as a people—said they would destroy every d——d Mormon. There was an army coming on the north and south, and it created some little excitement. I made two or three replies in a kind of debate of measures that were taken into consideration, discussing the object, what method we thought best to take in regard to protecting the lives of the citizens.

"My objections were not coincided with. At last we touched upon the topic like this:  We should still keep quiet, and a dispatch should be sent to Governor Young to know what would be the best course.  The vote was unanimous.  I considered it so.  It seemed to be the understanding that on the coming morning or next day there should be a messenger dispatched.  I took some pains to inquire and know if it would be sent in the morning.  The papers were said to .be made out, and Governor Young should be informed, and no hostile course pursued till his return.  I returned back to Fort Johnson, feeling that all was well. About eight and forty hours before the messenger returned, business called me to Cedar City, and I learned that the *job had been done*, that is the destruction of the emigrants had taken place.  I can't give any further evidence on the subject at present.

"What was the name of the messenger sent to Salt Lake?

"James Haslam."

I will now read to you the testimony of James Haslam:

"James Haslam, of Wellsville, Cache Valley, was sworn.  He lived in Cedar City in 1857; was ordered by Haight to take a message to President Young with all speed; knew the contents of the message; left Cedar City on Monday, September 7, 1857, between 5 and 6 p. m., and arrived at Salt Lake on Thursday at 11 a. m.; started back at 3 p. m., and reached Cedar about 11 a. m. Sunday morning, September 13th; delivered the answer from President Young to Haight, who said it was too late.  Witness testified that when leaving Salt

Lake to return, President Young said to him: 'Go with all speed, spare no horseflesh. The emigrants must not be meddled with, if it takes all Iron County to prevent it. They must go free and unmolested.' Witness knew the contents of the answer. He got back with the message the Sunday after the massacre and reported to Haight, who said, 'It is too late.'"

That is the testimony of James Haslam at the second Lee trial. According to what I have shown you President Young could not have been an accessory before the fact. He knew nothing about this matter until the dispatch came from Haight. As soon as he received that dispatch he sent back word —and told the messenger to spare no horseflesh in returning—that the emigrants must not be meddled with, and that if it took all Iron County to prevent them being interrupted by the Indians, it must be used for their protection. That is the testimony of James Haslam.

We have been tantalized a great deal in regard to the dispatch or letter sent by President Young by this messenger Haslam. As I had never seen it published I supposed that it could not be found. I had learned from President Young's testimony that the letter sent to him from Haight by Haslam was lost. But the evidence is clear that he sent a dispatch in reply to Haight at that time, and since President Young usually kept a copy of his correspondence, I supposed that this dispatch or a copy of it was in existentence. The *Tribune* of this city,

over and over again, has challenged the "Mormons"
to produce a copy of the dispatch or letter that
Brigham Young sent by James Haslam. James
Haslam testified that he delivered the dispatch to
Haight, but Haight said it was too late. But it is
objected, "Why don't you produce the dispatch?"
Now, I have taken pains to hunt this matter up,
and succeeded in getting the letter-book in which
the correspondence of President Young at that period was copied, and found this identical dispatch in
its order of date, and I am going to read it to you
tonight. I read the letter myself in the copying-
book, from Aug. 20, 1856 to Jan. 6, 1858, filed away
in the President's office; I have obtained a certified
copy of it and I know that it is correct:

PRESIDENT'S OFFICE.
GREAT SALT LAKE CITY, Sept. 10, 1857.
*Elder Isaac C. Haight:*

DEAR BROTHER:—Your note of the 7th inst.
is to hand. Capt. Van Vliet, Acting Commissary,
is here, having come in advance of the army to
procure necessaries for them. We do not expect
that any part of the army will be able to reach here
this fall. There is only about 850 men coming.
They are now at or near Laramie. A few of their
freight trains are this side of that place, the advance
of which are now on Green River. They will not
be able to come much if any further on account of
their poor stock. They cannot get here this sea-
son without we help them. So you see that the
Lord has answered our prayers, and again averted
the blow designed for our heads. In regard to the

emigration trains passing through our settlements, we must not interfere with them until they are first notified to keep away. You must not meddle with them. The Indians we expect will do as they please, but you should try and preserve good feelings with them. There are no other trains going south that I know of. If those who are there will leave, let them go in peace. While we should be on the alert, on hand, and always ready, we should also possess ourselves in patience, preserving our selves and property, ever remembering that God rules. He has overruled for our deliverance thus once again, and He will always do so if we live our religion and be united in our faith and good works.

All is well with us. May the Lord bless you and all the Saints forever.

Your brother in the gospel of Christ.

BRIGHAM YOUNG.

TERRITORY OF UTAH, } ss:
County of Salt Lake. }

I, Nephi W. Clayton, a notary public. within and for the County of Salt Lake, Territory of Utah, hereby certify that the foregoing is a full, true and correct copy of an impression of the foregoing letter; as witness my hand and official seal, at my office in Salt Lake City, Utah, this 18th day of October, A. D. 1884.

NEPHI W. CLAYTON,
Notary Public, Salt Lake County, U. T.

That is a full and verbatim copy of the letter sent by President Young in the hands of James Haslam to Isaac C. Haight, which arrived, as has been testified, forty-eight hours after the massacre. He reached Cedar City on Sunday, the 13th. The

massacre then took place on September 11th, the
day after this letter was written. Isaac C. Haight
said. "It is too late." He had sent for instructions,
accordind to the agreement in council, but had been
prevailed upon by John D. Lee to hurry the thing
up and not wait for a reply. John D. Lee said he
never heard of this letter until after he returned
from the Meadows. But it is clear that a letter was
sent. It is evident that Haight had written to President Young to find out how near the army was,
and what prospects there were of its coming here.
He had undoubtedly referred to this emigrant train,
and he informed the President of the antagonism
that prevailed against the emigrants on the part of
the Indians, and, in the answer, President Young
emphatically declared that the emigrants must not
be meddled with. This is strictly in accordance
with the instructions that I have shown you this
evening were given by President Young during
the whole of that period, that exciting time when
the army was coming, namely, to "shed no blood."
That was the counsel of the President. and that is
corroborated by this dispatch.

I do not think I need to spend any more time in
proving that President Young was not an accessory
before the fact. I believe it will be conceded by
everybody that understands these facts, that Brigham Young did not order the massacre; that he
was not implicated in it at all; that he did all in his
power to have these emigrants go through free and

in peace. I think this evidence is complete. It is
to me; and I have looked into this matter very
closely for my own information, and that I might lay
it before my friends.

Now, as to President Young being an accessory
after the fact. It is claimed that Lee came to Salt
Lake City, as directed by Haight, about the latter
part of September, to make a full and complete report of the massacre to President Young; to tell
who was there; and to give the names of the white
men who were engaged in the tragedy. The
question arises, is that true? Is it a fact that President Young was informed that John D. Lee and
other white men were engaged in that awful massacre? I hope you will be patient while I go into
that part of the subject and make this thing complete; for it is an important matter, we ought to
understand it, and the name of President Young
ought to be cleared from this stigma, if the story
is untrue. If it is true the responsibility should be
placed upon him, it doesn't belong to the "Mormon"
Church. If Brigham Young was guilty of any
complicity in this crime we want to know it, and I
do not shrink the investigation of anything. If
there is anything about this Church that cannot be
investigated I want to know it. But everything I
know about "Mormonism" will bear the light of
day. Everything I know of "Mormonism" will
bear investigation in the light of eternal truth, and
so with its relation to the subject before us tonight.

I know it, for I have looked at it in its bearings, in all its details, and I am not afraid to investigate anything pertaining to it.   If there is anything that will not stand investigation it is not worthy of credence, not fit to be a part of our faith and practice.   Then let us examine this matter and see if President Young was an accessory after the fact.   I will read from Bishop's book, page 252.   Here is John D. Lee's statement:

"According to the orders of Isaac C. Haight, I started to Salt Lake City to report the whole facts connected with the massacre to Brigham Young. I started about a week or ten days after the massacre, and I was on the way about ten days."

Now remember the massacre took place, according to the testimony, on the 11th day of September, 1857, for this reason: Haslam reached Cedar City on the Sunday, forty-eight hours after the massacre.   Everyone who has testified about it agrees that it took place on a Friday.   The Friday before the 13th was the 11th.   John D. Lee started for Salt Lake City about a week or ten days after the massacre and was about ten days on the road. That would bring him here about the end of September.   I will read Lee's statement again:

"According to the orders of Isaac C. Haight, I started for Salt Lake City to report the whole facts connected with the massacre to Brigham Young. I started about a week or ten days after the massacre, and I was on the way about ten days.   When I arrived in the city I went to the President's house and gave to Brigham Young a full, detailed statement of the whole affair, from first to last—only I took rather more on myself than I had done.

"He asked me if I had brought a letter from Haight, with his report of the affair. I said:

"'No; Haight wished me to make a verbal report of it, as I was an eye-witness to much of it.'

"I then went over the whole affair and gave him as full a statement as it was possible for me to give. I described everything about it. I told him of the orders Haight first gave me. I told him everything."

That is the statement of John D. Lee published after his death. Whether he said that or not I am not prepared to state; but it is published here, and we have to take it for what it is worth. We have seen a good many conflicting "confessions of John D. Lee," and that is one of them. Suppose it is true—although there is a doubt in my mind—that he claimed to have told President Young everything. This is the testimony of a being who is said to have brained a woman, who, it is proved cut a man's throat, shot wounded emigrants, whom he had decoyed out of their camp with a flag of truce. That is his testimony. Now, let us take the testimony of a man whose evidence is worthy of credence. I have two or three documents here. I will read you a statement made to me by President Wilford Woodruff, to which I got him to certify. Brother Woodruff is an honest, upright, truthful man, whose word can be relied upon implicitly. Is he not? I am sure everybody who

knows him will answer "Yes."   Here is his statement:

TERRITORY OF UTAH, } ss:
County of Salt Lake. }

Personally appeared before me the undersigned,
a notary public in and for said county, Wilford
Woodruff, who, being duly sworn, on his oath deposes and says:   I am a citizen of the United
States and a resident of Utah Territory, over the
age of twenty-one years.   In the fall of 1857 I was
in the office of Governor Brigham Young, in Salt
Lake City, when John D. Lee, who had just arrived
from the south, and was dusty and tired, came to
the front office and asked for a private interview
with Governor Young.   He was invited by the
Governor to the back office, I was requested to
accompany him.   We all went into the back office.
There John D. Lee made a statement concerning
the massacre of emigrants that had then recently
taken place at Mountain Meadows.   He stated that
the emigrants had aroused the hostility of the Indians by poisoning several springs from which the
Indians obtained water for drinking purposes; that
they had poisoned cattle which had died, by putting
poison into the carcasses, and that some of the Indians, who had eaten of the meat, died from its
effects; that in consequence of this and their vile
acts, the ire of the Indians was aroused, that he
could not restrain them.   He held them back as
long as he could, until the emigrants arrived at the
Mountain Meadows, when he could hold them back
no longer, and they attacked these emigrants and
killed them all except some small children.   Governor Young was profoundly affected.   He shed
tears and said that he was sorry that innocent blood

had been shed within the limits of this Territory. John D. Lee remarked, "There was not a drop of innocent blood in the camp." Governor Young asked indignantly, "What do you call the blood of women and children?" Lee was silent. Lee did not intimate by a single word that any white man had anything whatever to do with the massacre. He laid the whole thing to the Indians, and claimed that he had done his best to prevent the occurrence. In the fall of 1870 I was with President Brigham Young on a tour of the southern settlements. Erastus Snow who was then in charge of those settlements, informed President Young, as I then learned, that there were evidences of a strong character showing that John D. Lee was personally implicated in the Mountain Meadaws massacre. President Young was very much surprised, and declared that if it was true, John D. Lee had lied to him. When the President and company returned to Salt Lake City, he called a council of the President and the Twelve Apostles, when the matter was investigated, Elder Erastus Snow assisting in presenting the evidence; and the council unanimously voted to excommunicate John D. Lee for assisting in the murders at Mountain Meadows, and Isaac C. Haight, who was then President of the Stake in which Lee resided, for not restraining and preventing his participation in the crime. It was not until this occurrence last related, that President Young and his immediate associates fully realized the facts of Lee's guilt. Some had heard rumors of this, but the facts had not been brought to the President.

WILFORD WOODRUFF.

Subscribed and sworn to before me by the above-

named affiant, this 24th day of October, A. D.
1884.
[SEAL.]            NEPHI W. CLAYTON,
                        Notary Public.

After getting this affidavit from Brother Woodruff I said to him: "Brother Woodruff, you are
credited with keeping a regular journal of all important events in your history."

"Yes," said he, "I have got a large trunk full
of books comprising my journal."

"Well," said I, "you must have some record of
this occurrence that you have related to me."

He said he thought it quite likely. He looked
among his books and succeeded in finding the journal of that period and brought it to me. It is an
old book a little over an inch thick, and the writing
in his own peculiar. hand. I extracted from it
(under date of September 29, 1857,) all I could find
in relation to this matter, and I will give you my
affidavit:

TERRITORY OF UTAH, |
    County of Salt Lake. | ss:

Personally appeared before me the undersigned,
a notary public in and for said county, Charles W.
Penrose, who on his oath deposes and says: I am
a citizen of the United States over the age of
twenty-one years, and a resident of Salt Lake
County. I have obtained from Wilford Woodruff
of this city, a volume containing his journal from
January 1, 1854, to December, 1859, in his own
handwriting, with which I am acquainted. Under
date of September 29, 1857, I find the following:

"We have another express in this morning, saying that the army are rapidly marching toward us, will soon be at Bridger, and wish men immediately sent out. John D. Lee also arrived from Harmony with an express and an awful tale of blood. A company of California emigrants, of about 150 men, women and children. Many of them belonged to the mobbers of Misouri and Illinois. They had many cattle and horses with them, and they traveled along south. They went damning Brigham Young, Heber C. Kimball and the heads of the Church; saying that Joseph Smith ought to have been shot a long time before he was. They wanted to do all the evil they could, so they poisoned beef. and gave it to the Indians, and some of them died; they poisoned the springs of water, and several of the Saints died. The Indians became enraged at their conduct and they surrounded them on the prairie, and the emigrants formed a bulwark of their wagons, and dug an entrenchment up to the hubs of their wagons, but the Indians fought them five days until they had killed all the men, about sixty in number. They then rushed into the corral and cut the throats of the women and children, except some eight or ten children which they brought and sold to the whites. They stripped the men and women naked and left them stinking in the sun. When Brother Lee found it out he took some men and went and buried their bodies. It was a horrid, awful job. The whole air was filled with an awful stench. The Indians obtained all the cattle and horses and property, guns, etc. There was another large company of emigrants who had 1,000 head of cattle, who was also damning both the Indians and the 'Mormons.' They were afraid of sharing the same fate. Brother Lee had to send

interpreters with them to the Indians to help save
their lives, while at the same time they were trying
to kill us.   I spent most of the day in trying to get
the brethren ready to go to the mountains.   Brother
Brigham, while Lee was speaking of the cut-
ting of the throats of women and children by the Indians down south, said it was heart-rending; that
emigration must stop, as he had said before.   Brother
Lee said he did not think there was a drop of
innocent blood in the camp, for he had two of the
children in his house, and he could not get but one
to kneel down in prayer-time, and the other would
laugh at her for doing it, and they would swear
like pirates."

The foregoing extract is copied verbatim by
me from the journal of said Wilford Woodruff.

CHARLES W. PENROSE.

Subscribed and sworn to before me by the above-
named affiant, this 25th day of October, A. D.
1884.

[SEAL.]                NEPHI W. CLAYTON,
                              Notary Public.

I have read that extract from Brother Woodruff's journal because it completely corroborates
what he so clearly gave me from memory.   I will
now read you the affidavit of Brother John W.
Young:

TERRITORY OF UTAH, }
  County of Salt Lake { ss:

Personally appeared before me, the undersigned, a notary public, in and for said county, John
W. Young, who, on his oath, deposes and says: I
am a citizen of the United States, over the age of
twenty-one years.   In the fall of the year 1857, I

being then 13 years of age, was engaged at the
office of my father, Governor Brigham Young, as
messenger.  I distinctly remember one day in the
latter part of September, 1857, being at my father's
office when John D. Lee, travel-worn, as if he had
come in haste from a long journey, entered the
office and asked for a private interview with Gov.
Young.  He was shown into the back office, Elder
Wilford Woodruff going in with him.  I followed
them and heard the conversation.  It was custom-
ary for me to be present during those exciting
times when messengers arrived, so as to be ready
to carry any message that might have to be sent.
I do not remember that anyone else was present.

It is distinctly impressed on my mind beyond
the power of time to efface, how Lee described the
deed which he said was committed by the Indians
at Mountain Meadows.  He told of the depredations committed by the company of emigrants destroyed; how they poisoned meat and gave it to
the Indians, and also poisoned springs in their way,
by which several persons were killed.  Declared
that he tried to pacify the Indians, but they were
so enraged against the emigrants that it was impossible to prevent their attack.  He related how
the Indians killed the men and then butchered the
women, none being saved except a number of little
children, which he, Lee, was instrumental in rescu-
ing.  Also that he took men to help to bury the
dead.  Gov. Young was greatly moved.  I saw
him wipe away the tears as he listened to the
recital.  He expressed his horror at the deed, and
the shedding of innocent blood in this Territory.
Lee declared that no innocent blood was shed, for
the emigrants were a corrupt and murderous set.
Gov. Young referred to the women and children

who were slain, and declared that it was an awful crime. I was present during the whole interview, and know that Lee laid the matter entirely to the Indians, claiming that they alone killed the emigrants, against his earnest efforts to prevent it; that he was on the spot only to restrain the Indians and save life, and afterwards to bury the dead. He did not utter a syllable or convey any idea that either he or any other white person had any hand in the deed. The interview on that September morning impressed my boyish mind very strongly. Lee's recital was so forcible regarding the crime being committed by the Indians, and his sorrow and tears at the occurrence, appeared so sincere, that, years after, when it was rumored that white men were engaged in the massacre, I could not, and did not, believe it. It was only when proofs were brought which led to John D. Lee's excommunication from the Church, that I believed in his guilt. I was present on several occasions at the office of Gov. Young during the time of the approach of the army and heard Gov. Young warn those who had anything to do with the troops sent to intercept the army, to be careful not to shed blood. This was many times repeated. I have been present when Indian chiefs came to Governor Young and asked to go out against the army. Gov. Young would not consent to the shedding of one drop of blood. I also distinctly remember a meeting after the coming in of the army, and after the return from the move south, at which Gov. Cumming and one or two of the United States judges appointed with him were present, when the report that white men had been engaged in the massacre at Mountain Meadows was referred to, and President Young offered to go with the

governor and one of the judges—Cradlebaugh, I
believe, and help to fully investigate the matter,
and also to remain as a hostage in the hands of the
federal authorities, if necessary, until the investigation was made complete, so strong was his confi-
dence in the statement that none but Indians were
engaged in the massacre.

JOHN W. YOUNG.

Subscribed and sworn to before me by the above-
named affiant this 25th day of October, A. D.
1884.

[SEAL.]          NEPHI W. CLAYTON,
                     Notary Public.

I have yet another affidavit I want to present.
Some years ago in Ogden I had a conversation
with Judge Aaron Farr, who used to reside in Salt
Lake City, but for many years has resided in Ogden—a man of veracity, who was probate judge of
Weber County for many years. I was talking with
him about this deplorable affair and he told me
that after John D. Lee had made his report to
Brigham Young he (Lee), with whom he was
well acquainted, called at his house and saw him
and gave him an account of the massacre. I sent
word a few days ago to Judge Farr that I would
like his statement in writing, and here it is:

"I was personally acquainted with John D. Lee,
having known him when a boy in Nauvoo. In the
Fall of 1857, he came to Salt Lake City from his
home in Iron County, shortly after the massacre,
to report to Brigham Young how it occurred. On
the same day that he reported to President Young

in the morning, he came to my residence on West
Temple Street, opposite Bishop Hunter's place, in
the afternoon, and in a conversation with me, last-
ing about an hour and a half, detailed every particular of the horrible occurrence. He placed the
whole blame of the massacre on the Indians. He
stated that he and his associates had done all in
their power to protect the emigrants, but were
totally helpless in their object. He seemed very
earnest while he was telling me this story, and at
intervals wept bitterly. I asked him if he had informed President Young of these particulars, and
he answered me that he had seen President Young
that same morning and had related to him the
circumstances as he had told them to me."

AARON F. FARR, SEN.

UNITED STATES OF AMERICA, ⎫
    TERRITORY OF UTAH,      ⎬ ss:
        County of Weber.     ⎭
On this 23rd day of October, in the year of our
Lord one thousand eight hundred and eighty-four,
before me, Edward H. Anderson, a notary public,
within and for Weber County, in the Territory of
Utah, duly commissioned and qualified, personally
appeared Aaron F. Farr, Sen., who acknowledged
that the above statement to which his name is subscribed, is true.
In witness whereof I have hereunto set my seal
    in Ogden City, this the 23rd day of October,
    1884.

E. H. ANDERSON,
Notary Public, Weber County.

It appears to me that is pretty straight testimony. Place these three pieces of reliable evi-

dence against the statement of John D. Lee, the assassin, the butcher of women and children. Whose testimony would you receive if you were sitting on a jury? Would you believe the testimony of these three men of undoubted veracity, or the testimony of this cut-throat? I think you would prefer the testimony I have just read to you, at least I know I would, and I judge you by myself.

We are apt to measure other people's cloth by our yard-stick.

I will now read to you a very small portion of a letter to Secretary Belknap from President Young. The letter of President Young is under date of May 21, 1872. It is on file in the department at Washington:

"In 1858, when Alfred Cumming was Governor of Utah Territory, I pledged myself to lend him and the court every assistance in my power, in men and means, to thoroughly investigate the Mountain Meadows massacre and bring if possible the guilty parties to justice. *That offer I have made again and again,* and although it has not yet been accepted, I have neither doubt nor fear that the perpetrators of that tragedy will meet their just reward. But sending an armed force is not the means of furthering the ends of justice, although it may serve an excellent purpose in exciting popular clamor against the 'Mormons.' In 1859, Judge Cradlebaugh employed a military force to attempt the arrest of those alleged criminals. He engaged in all about four hundred men, some of whom were civilians, reputed gamblers, thieves, and other camp followers, who were doubtless

intended for jurors (as his associate, Judge Eccles,
had just done in another district); but these ac-
complished absolutely nothing further than plunder-
ing hen-roosts and rendering themselves obnoxious
to the citizens on their line of march. Had Judge
Cradlebaugh instead of peremptorily dismissing his
grand jury and calling for that military posse
allowed the investigation into the Mountain Meadows massacre to proceed, *I have the authority* of Mr.
Wilson, U. S. prosecuting attorney, for saying the
investigation was proceeding satisfactorily, and I
firmly believe, if the county sheriffs, whose legal
duty it was to make arrests, had been lawfully
directed to serve the processes, that they would
have performed their duty and the accused would
have been brought to trial. Instead of honoring
the law Judge Cradlebaugh took a course to screen
offenders, who could easily hide from such a posse
under the justification of avoiding a trial by court
martial.

"It is now fourteen years since the tragedy was
enacted and the courts have never tried to prosecute the accused; although some of the judges, like
Judge Hawley, have used every opportunity to
charge the crime upon prominent men in Utah,
and influence public opinion against our community."

Here is President Young's statement to the
Secretary of War at Washington, that he had
offered personally to Governor Cumming and Judge
Cradlebaugh to do all in his power to trace up the
massacre to its proper source. At that time Prest.
Young was firmly of the conviction that no white
man had been engaged in the massacre. The per-

petrators of the massacre were sworn to secrecy, as I have read to you. They were bound together not to tell. If anybody did tell he was to be killed. The mouths of those who knew were closed. President Young, therefore, had no idea that any white man was engaged in the deed; and when the rumor came that white men had been engaged in it he would not believe a word of it. And here we see that he offered to investigate the matter. Cradlebaugh came here at the time Governor Cumming came. He and Judge Eccles and Judge Sinclair were the three associate justices of Utah then appointed. Cradlebaugh was appointed to the southern district. He held his court at Provo, and he sent to Camp Floyd for the assistance of the military to help serve the processes of his court; but on an appeal being made to Governor Cumming to prevent the military from acting in this capacity, he issued his proclamation against this usurpation of the military, and because of this, the governor being sustained by the war department, and Cradlebaugh failing in his ulterior designs, no further effort was made to ferret out the criminals who were engaged in the Mountain Meadows massacre. The object of Judge Cradlebaugh was to criminate President Young; he did not care about anybody else, as I will prove to you from his own statement. I want you to pay particular attention to Judge Cradlebaugh's remarks:

"If it is expected that this court is to be used

by this community as a means of protecting it against the peccadilloes of Gentiles and Indians, unless this community will punish its own murderers, such expectations will not be realized. It will be used for no such purpose. When this people shall come to their reason, and manifest a disposition to punish their own high offenders, it will then be time to enforce the law also for their protection. If this court cannot bring you to a proper sense of your duty, it can, at least, turn the savages held in custody loose upon you."

This he proceeded to do, turning loose both Indians and white savages who had come into the Territory. His object was to try and implicate President Young, and have him arrested by this military posse, and brought before his court. Judge Sinclair tried the same thing here in this city, but did not succeed. Orders came from Washington that the military could not be used in executing the processes of civil courts, whereupon Judge Cradlebaugh, finding he could not implicate the authorities of the Church, nor force them before his court, got mad and turned loose all the criminals in custody in his district, as he describes them, "savages and others."

I will read to you now just a little extract from Stenhouse's book, page 401:

"The machinery of the courts was soon set in motion. The chief justice preferred the military camp for his residence. Associate Justice Sinclair was assigned to the district embracing Salt Lake City; and Associate Justice Cradlebaugh had within his district all the southern country.

"Up to this time the governor of the Territory had also been Superintendent of Indian affairs, but on the appointment of Governor Cumming, the office of Superintendent was conferred upon Jacob Forney, of Pennsylvania. Alexander Wilson, of Iowa, was appointed district attorney of the Territory, and thus was completed the full list of federal officials."

You will see that the office of governor went out of the hands of President Young about that time. When the army came in Cumming superseded him as governor, and Jacob Forney as agent of Indian affairs. But it is claimed that President Young was agent of Indian affairs at the time of the massacre, and ought to have reported this massacre to the authorities at Washington. Well, before he went out of office he did make a report. Let us see what it is like. It is published in Bishop's book:

OFFICE OF SUPT. OF INDIAN AFFAIRS,
G. S. L. CITY, Jan. 6th, 1858.

*Hon. James W. Denver, Commissioner of Indian Affairs, Washington City, D. C.:*

SIR:—On or about the middle of last September, a company of emigrants traveling the southern route to California, poisoned the meat of an ox that died and gave it to the Indians to eat, causing the immediate death of four of their tribe, and poisoning several others. This company also poisoned the water where they were encamped. This occurred at Corn Creek, fifteen miles south of Fillmore City. This conduct so enraged the Indians that they immediately took measures for revenge. I quote from a letter written to me by John D. Lee, farmer to the Indians in Iron and Washington Counties: "About the 22nd of September Captain Fancher & Co. fell victims to the Indians' wrath near Mountain Meadows. Their cattle and horses were shot down in every direction; their wagons and property mostly committed to the flames." Lamentable as this case truly is, it is only the natural consequence of that fatal policy which treated the Indians like wolves, or other ferocious beasts. I have vainly remonstrated for years with travelers against pursuing so suicidal a policy, and repeatedly advised the government of its fatal tend-· ency. It is not always upon the heads of the individuals who commit such crimes that such condign punishment is visited, but more frequently the next company that follows in their fatal path become the unsuspecting victims. though, peradventure, perfectly innocent.

On page 310 of the same book is the text of a letter to the same department, dated September 12, 1857, in which President Young advises some measures to be adopted, either to prevent the emigrants coming or to provide measures for their preservation.

Now, you see, Governor Young did report this as he was in duty bound to, and after making this report he was superseded, as I have told you, by Jacob Forney, as Indian agent.

I want to read to you now a word or two as to what Jacob Forney had to say on the subject. It appears on page 40 of Cradlebaugh's speech in

Congress, and is a report to the department at Washington:

"GREAT SALT LAKE CITY, Sept. 22, 1859.

"I gave,several months ago,to the attorney general and several of the United States judges, the names of those who I believe were not only implicated, but the hell-deserving scoundrels who concocted a part to the successful termination of the whole affair."

Thus,Jacob Forney made a report to the authorities at Washington, but no steps were taken to investigate the matter.

President Young then had gone out of office, both as governor and as superintendent of Indian affairs, and he was not responsible for any investigation in the matter in an official capacity. As you will perceive, there were some attempts made by the different governors and judges who rapidly succeeded each other, to show some interest in this affair. Their feeble efforts, however, were directed towards implicating President Young, and there was no real endeavor to convict the actual criminals ever made until Sumner Howard, U. S. district attorney for this Territory, prosecuted John D. Lee on his second trial. Previous to that all pretended efforts were directed towards criminating Brigham Young and the "Mormon" Church; no sincere movements were made to ferret out the persons who perpetrated this deed. President Young, not being acquainted with the facts in the matter, took no steps to punish Lee. He was profoundly impressed

with the idea that the deed had been perpetrated
by the Indians.    This explains the reason why
President Young, not now Governor Young, did
not exercise ecclesiastical authority in reference to
the assassin.    I will here read to you the, affidavit
of Hon. Erastus Snow, whose word no one who
knows him will dispute for a moment:

TERRITORY OF UTAH, }
   County of Salt Lake. } ss:

    Personally appeared before me,the undersigned,
a notary public in and for said county, Erastus
Snow, who, being first duly sworn, on his oath
says: I am a citizen of the United States, and resident of the Territory of Utah, over the age of 21
years.    That inasmuch as President B. Young has
been reproached for not expelling from the Church
of Jesus Christ of Latter-day Saints John D. Lee,
immediately after the Mountain Meadows massacre
instead of waiting until October 8th, 1870; the
reason was that President Young and other authorities of said Church in Salt Lake City were in
ignorance of the full facts relating to John D. Lee's
connection therewith; by the false representations
made by said Lee, as Indian farmer, to Governor
Brigham Young. to the effect that the Indians were
alone responsible for that slaughter, and that Lee
and others visited the scene in the interests of
peace, but were unable to restrain them.    After
colonies of our people began to locate in Washington County, in the years 1861, 1862 and 1863, and
I was sent there to preside over them, I began to
learn from various persons, little by little, the facts
in the case, which satisfied me that the said Lee
had taken a direct hand with the Indians in that

affair; and I felt it my duty to acquaint the Presidency of the Church with the facts so far as I had been able to gather them.

Bishop L. W. Roundy, of Kannarra, some ten miles from Lee's ranch, was also engaged as well as myself, in ferreting out the facts in relation thereto. President Young made a visiting tour through the southern part of the Territory in the Fall of the year 1870. I met him at Kannarra, on his downward trip, and took him and Bishop L. W. Roundy by themselves; Roundy is now dead; and communicated to President Young the facts as we had learned them, and the sources of our information. It made a profound impression on President Young; he expressed great astonishment, and said if such were the facts, Lee had added to his crime lying and deceit to him, and wondered how and why those facts had been so long concealed from him. On his return to Salt Lake City President Young called a council of the Twelve Apostles of the Church, and laid the facts before them, and President Young himself proposed, and all present unanimously voted to expel John D. Lee and Isaac C. Haight, who was his superior officer in the Church, for failing to restrain him, and to take prompt action against him, and President Young gave instructions at that time that John D. Lee should, under no circumstances, ever be again admitted as a member of the Church.

During the following Winter, while Presidents Brigham Young and George A. Smith were at my home in St. George, Lee made application to me to intercede for him to obtain an interview with them; but when I spoke to them about it they both positively declined to see him or receive any communication from him.      ERASTUS SNOW.

Subscribed and sworn to before me, this 21st day of February, A. D. 1882.

[SEAL.]      JAMES JACK, Notary Public.

Now, you will see how the facts first came to the cognizance of President Young. Brother Erastus Snow was sent down to take charge of the southern country. There certain hints were given and things began to come out; he commenced to trace them up, and when he had gathered certain facts he laid them before President Young. It was found that Lee had added lying and deceit to his deeper crimes, and he was cut off the Church and denied re-admission.

Now, suppose that Lee was an accomplice of Brigham Young, that Brigham Young was an accessory either before or after the fact, would he have dared to take these steps against Lee or Haight? No. If Lee and Haight had received instructions from President Young, or the latter had palliated or condoned the crime, would Prest. Young have cut them off the Church of Jesus Christ of Latter-day Saints, and that without a remedy?

At Lee's first trial he was not convicted. The jury was composed partly of "Mormons" and partly of non-Mormons; but the jury disagreed. And if you had read the testimony as I have done, you would see that in refusing to bring in a verdict of

"guilty," they who did so were justified, because
the crime was not then clearly traced to Lee.    One
of the main objects of the prosecution then was to
implicate the higher ecclesiastical authorities of
the "Mormon" Church.    But, of course, they were
not on trial.    Mr. Baskin for the prosecution said:

"The country does not want to see that old
man hanged; it only wants to see the fair fame of
the country vindicated."

And he went on to arraign the "Mormon"
Church and Brigham Young as "commanding men
to murder and spoliate."    And it is admitted in the
*Tribune* report of that trial, page 6, that

"The prosecuting officers, in dealing with this
great crime, were less desirous to convict and punish the prisoner than to get at the long-concealed
facts of that case.    The impression that there was
'some person (or persons), high in the estimation
of the people,' at the bottom of the affair, had
grown to be a settled conviction; and as Lee had
been a subordinate actor in the massacre it was
thought that the ends of justice would be attained
by releasing this man if he was honest in his
avowed resolution to tell it all."

At the second trial the evidence was plain and
direct as to Lee's complicity in the massacre; he
was convicted by "Mormon" testimony, and a verdict of "guilty" was brought in against him by a
"Mormon" jury—I have a list of their names,* all

*—Wm. Greewood, John E. Page, A. M. Farnsworth,
Stephen S. Barton, Valentine Carson, Alfred I. Randall, James
S. Montague, A. S. Goodwin, Ira B. Elmer, Andrew A. Correy,
Charles Adams and Walter Granger.

members of the "Mormon" Church. Strange thing, was it not, to have a "Mormon" jury? It would be singular in these times. But John D. Lee was convicted by a "Mormon" jury, a thing said by some of the newspapers, extracts from which I have read to you, to be "impossible."

All this goes to show to this audience and to the world that the charge of this massacre cannot be laid to the "Mormon Church," to George A. Smith, to Brigham Young or to the Twelve Apostles; it can only be laid to John D. Lee and such white men who were present on that occasion and who participated in the massacre. But it is very evident from the testimony, both on the first and on the second Lee trial, that but few white men fired a gun. Most of the massacre was done by the Indians, who were armed, some of them with guns and some with bows and arrows. I could bring you a mass of testimonies given at the two trials to show how these white men came to go to the Meadows; that they were "lured" by Haight, and Lee, and Klingensmith. They were told to go there with guns and spades; that the Indians had attacked the emigrants, and that they were wanted to help bury the dead, and protect the emigrants. They were not told to go there and kill the emigrants, and it is very clear that very few of them took any active part in the massacre. After the terrible deed was done, however, they were all sworn to secrecy, and kept their oaths for awhile.

But the thing began to leak out. It was too horrible, too wicked, too much against their religion to keep. Every person who belongs to the Church of Jesus Christ of Latter-day Saints, and understands the doctrines of the Church, and has a particle of the spirit of this gospel, knows that it is not the spirit of its members to shed blood, knows that the doctrines of the Church teach to the contrary, and that it is looked upon as the very worst of crimes for a man to kill his fellow-man. As I showed you two weeks ago in a discourse on "blood atonement," there were certain capital sins that could not be atoned for except by the shedding of the person's own blood, and that after a person has received certain ordinances and made certain covenants, and then commits murder he cannot be forgiven in this world or in the world to come. That is the doctrine of this Church.

How, then, can this people be accused of complicity in a crime which is right against their feelings, contrary to their faith, prohibited by the revelations, which they believe to be the revelations of God, opposed to the public teachings and the private instructions of the leaders of the Church right in the face of the positive injunctions of those leaders not to shed blood under any circumstances except in self-defense.

I think I have made out a case that Brigham Young was not an accessory after the fact. I will have to pass over some items I would like to have brought before the congregation, all in this same line of argument; but I will skip them owing to the lateness of the hour. It was said that some property was brought into Salt Lake City from Mountain Meadows, and that Brigham Young got possession of it, while Captain Hooper bought the stock. Allow me to read a little more from Bishop, page 268. Here is what John D. Lee said after he was condemned to death:

"But is there no help'for the widow's son? I can no longer expect help from the Church or those of the Mormon faith. If *I escape execution* it will be through the clemency of the nation, many of whose noble sons will dislike to see me sacrificed in this way. I acknowledge that I have been slow to listen to the advice of friends, who have warned me of the danger and treachery that awaited me, yet I ask pardon for all the ingratitude with which I received their advice. When the people consider that I was ever taught to look upon treachery with horror, and that I have never permitted one nerve or fibre of this old frame to weaken or give way, notwithstanding I have been cut loose, and cast off and sacrificed by those who from their own standpoint, and according to their own theory, should have stood by me to the last, they may have some compassion for me. Perhaps all is for the best."

You see there is an intimation in that, that he thought he might perhaps escape punishment. There was considerable reason perhaps for that. It is stated that there was an agreement made between John D. Lee and Sumner Howard, the prosecuting attorney, and Mr. Nelson who was then U. S. Marshal, and is now one of the editors of the *Salt Lake Tribune*, that John D. Lee should make out these documents that they might publish them to the world and make money out of it; but I will not enter into the evidences of that tonight. But John D. Lee had an idea that perhaps there was a loop-hole through which he might escape. His first confession did not suit. He made up a "confession" at the first trial for Messers Carey and Baskin who were the prosecuting attorneys on that occasion, and it was supposed that that confession would save a great deal of trouble at that trial. The substance of that confession is published in this *Tribune* pamphlet. After giving an account of the massacre the report says:

"But the statement goes no further in its implication than the local leaders who directed the butchery, and totally fails to throw light upon the complicity of the higher ecclesiasts from whom the order emanated."

It was for that reason it did not suit, for, as I have already shown you, the real object at that trial was if possible to criminate Brigham Young. Now I want to read to you a short paragraph from Mr. Howard's statement at the next trial, when John D. Lee was convicted:

"District Attorney Howard opened the case to the jury for the prosecution. He reviewed the history of the case, and announced that he came there to try John D. Lee, and not Brigham Young, and the Mormon Church, who were not indicted. He intended to try John D. Lee for acts committed by Lee personally. He recited to the jury the facts which he proposed to prove by competent testimony as to John D. Lee's guilt in the case."

After he had made his opening speech, Mr. W. W. Bishop, the publisher of this book, said:

"He was glad to hear that Brigham Young and the Mormon Church were not on trial in this case. It was the first time in Utah that he had the pleasure of trying the case on its own merits."

Mr. Bishop here acknowledges that the attempt before was merely to implicate Brigham Young and the "Mormon" Church; but now John D. Lee was on his trial on his own merits. The "Mormon" Church and Brigham Young were not then on trial.

At the close of the second trial U. S. District Attorney Sumner Howard,

"In his opening address, repeated again that he had come for the purpose of trying John D. Lee, because the evidence led and pointed to him as the main instigator and leader, and he had given the jury unanswerable documentary evidence, proving that the authorities of the Mormon Church knew nothing of the butchery until after it was committed, and that Lee, in his letter to President Young a few weeks later, had knowingly misrepresented the actual facts relative to the massacre, seeking to keep him still in the dark and in ignorance.

"He had received all the assistance any United States official could ask on earth in any case. Nothing had been kept back, and he was determined to clear the calendar of every indictment against any and every actual guilty participator in the massacre, but he did not intend to prosecute any one that had been lured to the meadows at that time, many of whom were only young boys and knew nothing of the vile plan which 'Lee originated and carried out for the destruction of the emigrants."

Now, in regard to what became of the property said to have been taken from Mountain Meadows, I will refer to John D. Lee's statement, page 245:

"The bodies were all searched by Higbee, Klingensmith and Wm. C. Stewart. I did hold the hat awhile, but I soon got so sick that I had to give it to some other person, as I was unable to stand for a few minutes. The search resulted in getting a little money and a few watches, but there was not much money. Higbee and Klingensmith kept the property, I suppose, for I never knew what became of it, unless they did keep it. I think they kept it all."

It was currently reported that Brigham Young gobbled it all. In regard to the cattle that Capt. Hooper was supposed to have obtained. It was stated in Congress that Hooper had the cattle that came from the Mountain Meadows. I will read from page 292:

"My worthy attorney, W. W. Bishop, will please insert it in my record or history, should I not be able to write up my history to the proper place, to speak of my worthy friend, Wm. H. Hooper. Please exonerate him from all blame or censure of buying the stock of that unfortunate company, as there is *no truth* in the accusation whatever."

On page 250, Lee declares Klingensmith sold these cattle; that he and Haight kept all the proceeds and started a mercantile business with it in Cedar City. I give that for what it may be worth, but it goes to disprove that Brigham Young obtained any of the ill-gotten property.

John D. Lee was taken to the Mountain Meadows and there shot for the crime committed, on the 23rd of March, 1877. This was done for dramatic effect. It is between 80 and 90 miles from Beaver, where he was convicted. I do not think that such a thing as moving a criminal for execution to the spot where his crime was committed was ever done before within the limits of the United States. If it has been I am not aware of it. But the object of it was to make the book sell a little better. The book is a dramatic one, and the crime to which it related was made to have a dramatic termination.

I will now read to you a few words taken down from the lips of President John Taylor in regard to this matter. I want you to understand his sentiments in regard to this affair. It was written in the winter of 1882:

"I now come to the investigation of a subject

that has been harped upon for the last seventeen years, namely the Mountain Meadows massacre. That bloody tragedy has been the chief stock-in-trade for penny-a-liners, and press and pulpit, who have gloated in turns by chorus over the sickening details. 'Do you deny it?' No. 'Do you excuse it?' No. There is no excuse for such a relentless, diabolical, sanguinary deed. That outrageous infamy is looked upon with as much abhorrence by our people as by any other parties in this nation or in the world, and at its first announcement its loathing recital chilled the marrow and sent a thrill of horror through the breasts of the listeners. It was most certainly a horrible deed, and like many other defenseless tragedies, it is one of those things that cannot be undone. The world is full of deeds of crime and darkness, and the question often arises, Who is responsible therefor? It is usual to blame the perpetrators. It does not seem fair to accuse nations, states and communities for deeds perpetrated by some of their citizens, unless they uphold it."

I have read this that you may know the sentiments of the present President of the Church in regard to this crime, and I think his sentiments will be endorsed by every Latter-day Saint.

I have read to you tonight a number of the stories circulated in regard to this matter, laying this massacre to the body of the "Mormon" Church. In the beginning of my remarks I read copiously from papers published in different parts of the world, showing that the crime was broadly charged to the Latter-day Saints. I might also read to you from the Salt Lake *Tribune,* but I will not detain you. That paper has over and over again laid this crime at the door of the "Mormon" Church. These bugaboo stories put me in mind a great deal of the boy's essay on pins. After several amusing remarks about those useful articles, he said they had been "the means of saving thousands of human lives, by reason of their not swallowing of them." Whenever these stories *are* swallowed they produce poisonous effects. They are injurious to the vision. And that is the object for which they are used, that the eyes of the people may be blinded, so that when the Elders go forth with the gospel of Christ, people, being blinded through prejudice, will not be willing to receive it. The clergy have helped to spread abroad these infamous stories. I think I have proved tonight that the "Mormon" people are not guilty of this massacre in any way; that the "Mormon" Church, as an organization, is not responsible for it; that George A. Smith merely went south, as some did to the north, to warn the people in regard to the waste of grain and flour, and other provisions; that he did not speak against this company of emigrants at all, for he did not know of their existence until he was on his way back. I think I have proved to you that Brigham Young was not an accessory before the fact, nor an accessory after the fact; that when the facts came to the knowledge of President Young he then and there excommunicated John D. Lee and Isaac C.

Haight from the Church and would not allow them to enter again; that Brigham Young's name stands today clear from the guilt which malignant people have tried to fasten upon it. Brigham Young was not a man of blood, nor even a warrior, but a philanthropist and a statesman—a statesman of a very high order. His soul did not delight in physical conflict, nor in the shedding of blood. I could produce to you to-night sermon upon sermon from the *Journal of Discourses* in which he deprecates the shedding of blood. I could produce to you to-night, as I did two weeks ago, his teachings concerning the awful penalties attached to the shedding of the blood of a human being ; and I think all this mass of testimony produced to-night goes to prove that neither Brigham Young nor the Church either authorized, or countenanced, or palliated, or excused in the least degree the horrible massacre at Mountain Meadows.

And now I will bring to a close my remarks. Let us investigate. Let us be a thinking people, a reading people, a people that think for ourselves, a people that will not be led away by any story that may be spread abroad in the world. And let us help to send forth the truth. I think we have been a little to blame in this matter. We have been continually assailed. Our enemies have told some of the most monstrous stories that it is capable for the mind of man to invent, his tongue to repeat or devils inspire him to pen. I think we should take a stand to expose these falsehoods, to defeat this influence, to place ourselves on record against them. I think the people called Latter-day Saints should use the pen and the press to scatter truth broadcast in the world. We do not expect to meet all the lies they tell of us. A man can ask questions and bring forth by implication as much in an hour as would take ten years to refute. If we cannot reply to all the lies that are told about us, we can, at least, endeavor to do our best in refuting some of the worst. It is our duty to do so. We have been warned; now let us warn our neighbors. We have got the truth; let us spread it abroad. By the help of God we will labor to this end. I devoted myself to the work of spreading the truth in my boyhood. I feel just the same to-day; and I know I have been blessed of God in this labor. I know the Spirit and power of God are in this Church. I know this is the work of God. I know God has established it, and I know He will bring it to a glor- ious consummation. I know that all the lies the engines of destruction and all the influences, physical, or moral, or intellectual, that may be brought against this Church will ultimately fail. "Truth is mighty and will prevail." And while I live, by the help of God, I shall endeavor to do my part, both by tongue and pen, in defending my brethren and sisters and the servants of God in this Church from the malicious attacks and calumnies of their opponents, and in preaching the gospel of peace to the ends of the earth. To this I have consecrated my life, and doing this I have done but the same as many others. I know my words find an echo in your hearts. You know as well as I do that this is the spirit of this Church, that the spirit of our leaders, the First Presidency, the Apostles and our leading men is peace. Our motto is "Peace on earth, good-will to all men." Our mission is salvation, not destruction. We come to save men's lives, not to destroy them.

May God help us to labor in this spirit and give us strength and faith that we may accomplish the work unto which we are called, for Christ's sake. Amen.

# SUPPLEMENT.

## TESTIMONY OF JAMES HOLT HASLAM.

TAKEN AT WELLSVILLE, CACHE COUNTY, UTAH,
DECEMBER 4, 1884.

JAMES HOLT HASLAM, being interrogated by S. A. Kenner, Esq., answered the interrogatories to him propounded as follows:

What is your full name?

James Holt Haslam.

And where do you now reside?

In Wellsville, Cache County, Utah.

How long have you resided in this Territory?

Since the Fall of 1851.

Have you been here continuously from that time?

You mean in Utah?

Yes.

Yes, sir.

In what part of Utah were you residing in the year 1857?

In the year 1857 I was residing at Cedar City, in Iron County.

What part of Iron County?

Cedar City.

Do you remember September of that year?

I remember it well.

Do you remember the incident in the history of Utah known as the Mountain Meadows massacre or murder?

Yes, sir.

What time of the year did it occur?

It was in September.

In 1857 or 1858?

In 1857.

Did you perform any office or any service in connection with those engaged in that transaction?

All that I performed was to carry an express from Cedar to Salt Lake City.

Who sent you on that errand?

Isaac C. Haight.

What position, if any, did he hold in that community where you lived?

President of Cedar City.

By virtue of what authority was he president, if you know?

No more than he was called to that office?

I mean under what dispensation or government?

Under the church government of the Church of Jesus Christ of Latter-day Saints.

Did he hold any other position?

I believe he was colonel of militia of what is called the Nauvoo Legion.

As the presiding officer of that community, were you subject to his order?

Yes, in a church capacity I was.

Do you remember the company of emigrants that were massacred at the Mountain Meadows?

I remember seeing them pass through Cedar City on their way south.

About what time was that with reference to your receiving this dispatch?

A few days after, I should say it must have been somewhere about the fifth or sixth of September, 1857.

Was it before or after you received the dispatch?

Oh, before I received the dispatch.

About how many days before?

I should judge from one to two days, but I could not say positively.

State now, as nearly as you can, considering the state and circumstances leading to Mr. Haight giving that dispatch and with orders to convey it there.

Word came up to Mr. Haight from John D. Lee, stating that the Indians had got the emigrants corralled on the Mountain Meadows, and wanted to know what he should do.

Who brought that word?

I don't know, I did not see the man who brought the word to Haight.

What did Mr. Haight tell you in relation to the matter at that time?

He sent for me. He had a message written to

send up to Brigham Young, and he wished to get a man to take it up. He had not found one when I went down there to his house, and he asked me if I would take it. I told him I would if it was possible to take it.

Did he then state the nature of that message that he wanted you to carry and deliver?

He gave me the message to read.

Did you read it?

Yes, sir.

State the contents of it as near as you possibly can.

The same as I stated before: that the Indians had got the emigrants corralled at the Mountain Meadows, and Lee wanted to know what should be done. Lee at this time was major of what was called the Post, and he was the Indian agent.

My question was in relation to the emigrants— what do you mean by the Post?

It was a fort and intended to devise means of protection from the Indians.

Was that message placed in an envelope and sealed?

Yes, sir.

To whom was it addressed?

To Brigham Young, governor of Utah Territory.

What did you do with it when you took possession of it?

I wrapped it up carefully and put it away where no one would get it until I delivered it.

How long after receiving it was it before you started for Salt Lake City?

Just as quick as I could go home, put on a shirt and saddle a horse.

About how far did you live from Haight's, or from where you received the message?

About a quarter of a mile.

How long did it take you to go and do that?

Probably from ten to fifteen minutes.

Is it a fact that after the receipt of that message you were in the saddle ready to depart and did depart within fifteen minutes from the time of its reception?

Yes, sir.

What kind of a horse did you start on.

A spanish horse.

Please state as to its fleetness.

I could not state as to that.

How long did it take you to arrive at Parowan?

I could not say exactly, might be about two hours.

What is the distance?

Between eighteen and twenty miles.

Did you proceed on the same horse from there?

Yes, sir, to Beaver.

Do you know about what time you arrived at Beaver?

To the best of my recollection now, Bishop P. T. Farnsworth was Bishop there, and to the best of my recollection, when I arrived at Beaver he said it was nine o'clock, or a little past in the evening.

Do you remember the time when you left Cedar?

A little past four o'clock in the afternoon.

Did you change horses at Beaver?

Yes, sir.

How long were you in effecting the change of horses?

While I was eating supper they got the horse and put the saddle on it.   They got the horse from Edward Thompson, Sen.

Did you state the nature of your mission to the Bishop?

I did, sir.

And he then proceeded immediately to get you a fresh horse?

Yes, sir.

So you immediately got on and went as fast as possible, did you?

Yes, sir; I got a note from Col. Dame to all the Bishops, stating my business, and for them to furnish me horses.

And it was by virtue of you showing this note that the Bishop at Beaver furnished you a horse?

Yes, sir.

Did you proceed immediately on your journey to Fillmore?

Right away.

How long did you ride after that?

From that to Fillmore.

Without stopping?

Without stopping, on the same horse, yes, on the same horse to Fillmore.

Can you remember the time you arrived at Fillmore—time of day or night?

I could not recollect exactly.

Can you remember how many hours?

No, sir; I got to Fillmore sometime before daylight, but I could not say exactly what time of the following day.

How long did you stay in Fillmore?

I had to stay till the Bishop came, and that was pretty near evening. He was off on a hunt, he and his horses too.

Who was Bishop there at that time?

Seymour Brunson.

Were you resting during this time?

I had to do: my horse could not go any further without urging him very much, as he had come from Beaver.

How long were you there waiting for the Bishop to arrive?

That day; and after he arrived I did not stop but a little while.

Did he get you a horse immediately?

Yes, sir; but it was a horse that I could only ride ten miles. I rode to Cedar Springs, or Holden.

Did you there obtain another horse?

They hadn't got one in Holden—had to send back to Fillmore and get another one.

How much time did that occupy?

That occupied, before they got back with another horse, till three o'clock in the morning next day.

Did you then immediately proceed?

Yes, sir.

How far did you go that time?

To Salt Creek, or Nephi.

In about what time did you make that journey?

I was there at seven o'clock in the morning.

And you obtained another horse there, did you?

Yes, sir.

How much time did that occupy there?

Just long enough to eat breakfast—not to exceed half an hour.

And you then proceeded northward?

Yes, sir.

How far did you go that time?

To Payson.

How long did you stay there?

Just long enough to change horses.

That would be but a few minutes?

That is all.

How far did you go next time?

To Provo.

Did you get another horse there?

Yes, sir.

How much time did you spend in Provo?

An hour.

Then proceeded on your journey again?

Yes, sir.

Where was your next stopping place.

At American Fork.

Did you get another horse there?

Yes, sir.

How long did you stay there?

Well, about half an hour.

And then went on continuously?

Went right on.

Where did you arrive at next?

I went right on to Salt Lake City from American Fork.

How long did it take you to go from American Fork to Salt Lake City?

I could not say exactly how long it was, but I went right on, yet got kind of sleepy that night.

What day of the week was it you arrived at Salt Lake City?

I can't remember that, but think it was Thursday morning.

Can you give me the time you occupied from Cedar City to Salt Lake City, altogether, including stoppages and everything?

I left Cedar at four o'clock in the afternoon, and it was the morning of the third day from then that I got to Salt Lake City.

After you left Cedar?

Yes, sir, I was at the Lion House just after

daybreak, where Brigham Young had his office, or it was then.

That would be, then, about sixty hours, would it not, on your journey?

Yes, sir, somewhere along there: two whole days and a little more than half of another.

Well, was it not about sixty hours?

Yes, about that time.

How many hours were taken up by these stoppages and delays altogether?

Well, about fifteen—yes, there was all of twenty hours taken up.

What was the first thing you did when you arrived at Salt Lake City?

To go to Brigham's office.

Did you see him there?

Yes, sir.

Immediately upon your arrival?

You might call it immediately. It was not over fifteen minutes.

Did you see him in his office?

Yes, sir.

What did you do when you first saw him?

I handed him my message.   .

Did you tell him whom you received it from?

Not until he asked me the question.

Did you then?

Yes, sir, I did.

What did he do?

He opened it and read it.

What, if anything, did he say after he read it?

He told me I had better go and lie down and take a little sleep.

What else, if anything?

He told me to be there again at such a time, and he would be ready to give me an answer.

Did he mention any time?

Yes, sir.

What time was it that he suggested?

One o'clock in the afternoon of the same day.

Were there any others present besides President Young on that occasion?

Yes, sir.

State, if you can recollect, who they were.

I can't recollect all, but Squire Wells, John Taylor, and I should think about as many as half a dozen.

Do you remember George Q. Cannon and John Taylor?

I cannot say whether George Q. was there or not; I cannot say as to him positively, because I don't recollect.

Mention as many as you can remember.

That is about as many as I can remember—Daniel H. Wells and John Taylor.

How many were there altogether?

I should think there was all of half a dozen or more in a council.

Was this at the time you first went in—who was there when you first went to President Young?

About how long were you on the road taking the message down and going to Cedar City?

About the same as I was coming up, as near as I can think.

What did Mr. Haight say to you when you handed him the message or answer and he read it?

He said, "Too late, too late." The massacre was all over before I got home.

Did he say anything further on that subject?

No, sir; he cried like a child.

How long were you in his company at that time?

About half an hour.

Did he make any further reference to the subject?

No, sir; he could not talk about it at all.

At what place was this, and where?

In Cedar City.

Was he at his home at the time you delivered this message to him?

No.

At what place was he?

Between his house and mine, on the way coming down to see if I had got back.

Did he, at that time or afterwards, say anything with reference to his being at the massacre or not?

Never to my knowledge.

Did you see John D. Lee then at that time?

No, sir, I did not.

Have you seen him since?

Yes, sir, many times.

How long after that before you saw him first?

About two weeks.

Did he make any reference to the subject?

No, sir.

Did you?

No, sir.

Have you at any time since that date heard him or Haight speak in reference to that subject?

No, sir.

Do you know John M. Higbee?

Yes, sir.

Have you ever heard him say anything about it?

No, sir.

Have you heard the subject discussed by any-one there or elsewhere about that time?

No more than common rumor since that date?

Have you ever heard Mr. Dame talk about it?

Nu, sir.

Do you know what became of that dispatch?

You mean the one I brought back?

Yes.

I do not.

Did you see what disposition Mr. Haight made of it?

He put it in his pocket after he read it.

Have you ever seen it since?

No, sir.

Have you ever heard it mentioned in Church meetings or anywhere else?

No, sir.

Was there at that time a telegraph line in the Territory?

No, sir.

What was the mail service, if any, through the Territory at that time, if you know?

Mails were carried just as it happened.

Was there a regular through mail?

The mail came now and then about as it happened, as near as I can remember. If anybody went up to Salt Lake City they would bring back what mail there was there.

About how often did the mail come there?

Only as it was brought, kind of promiscuous.

Did it come as often as once a month?

I don't think it did.

Was it any oftener than that?

No, sir, I don't think it was.

How long was it after that time that you next met President Young?

I can't say, for I don't recollect. I came up to Salt Lake City in 1859 and worked there till Fall; I can't remember any particular date.

But you have met him since?

Oh, yes, many times.

And heard him speak in places, in pulpits?

Yes, sir.

Have you ever heard him, in his house, in any place, or in any of the streets, or in any place of worship, or pulpit, or at any place whatever, make any reference to the subject that you have just testified to and under discussion?

I have.

Will you, according to your best recollection, give me, as near as possible, the nature of what he said at any of these places or times?

If I can recollect anything he said at all, he said it was one of the worst things that ever happened or could have happened in Utah, and those that had perpetrated that deed would go to hell for it. I have heard him use such an expression as that.

Then, to the best of your recollection, from what you have seen of him, what you have known of him, what you have heard him say, he was not only bitterly opposed to that whole proceeding, but discountenanced the men who engaged in it?

He did.

Do you know anything concerning any spoils or property that accrued from that massacre?

Only from hearsay.

Have you ever seen any of it?

Oh, yes.

In whose possession did you see it?

In John D. Lee's.

Did you ever see any in anybody else's possession?

I can't say that I did, unless they bought it from Lee.

Did you ever know or hear of Brigham Young having any property or money that was obtained from that affair at that time?

No, sir.

Did you ever hear of any having been offered him?

Only by report to me from a man that Lee told.

What was the nature of that report?

The nature was that Lee offered him money that he had got from that company, and he told him to take it out of his sight and not let him see him any more, didn't want to even see him, let alone the money; that is only common report.

Did you immediately after that?

Many times.

Do you know what his relations were after that with Brigham Young?

I do not; but as far as I know I don't believe there was any.

Do you know whether or not either ever visited the other after?

I don't know, but I don't believe they ever did.

You were in such a position at that time, were you not, that anything of that nature going on in the community would have most likely reached you, if it had taken place?

I think it would.

Were you in as good a position for knowing such things as other people at that time?

Yes, sir.

Do you know what the sentiment of the people of the Church was at that time—I mean those that you were intimately associated with—in relation to that affair?

Yes, sir; the sentiment was it never ought to have happened.

Have you heard members of the Church, in good standing, speak of it since?

Yes; that it never ought to have happened.

What was the state of the community at that time—at the time you took this dispatch to be carried to Salt Lake?

On the way through the Indians were very bad—they were excited, and they were up in arms on account of the treatment they had received from this company of emigrants.

Do you know anything of this treatment they complained of?

I know what the Indians told me when I was on the road carrying the dispatch.

State what it was.

They told me the emigrants had poisoned their water and had done everything that was mean for them, and that they were going to kill the emigrants for doing it.

Did the Indians at that time know the nature of your message?

Of what I was carrying?

Yes.

Yes, sir.

Did they oppose you in any way?

No more than to stop me and inquire if I was

going to see the "big captain," and I told them I
was. They wanted to know what it was about and
I told them they were not to kill the "Mericats,"
but to let them go about their business; for the
"big captain" would be angry with them if they
did it.

Who was meant by the "big captain?"

Brigham Young.

What did they say to that?

They said they should not do it; they were
mad and they were going to kill the emigrants.
They said they were going to do it before I came
back.

Can you remember the precise place where
this conversation with the Indians occurred?

The place was down between what was called
Cedar Ridge, or Pine Creek Hill, and Cove Creek.

How long, if you know, had it been before
that that the emigrants had passed there?

There was one company camped in Beaver.

When you were going up with the dispatch?

Yes, sir.

Were there any others ahead of them?

This company that was massacred at the
Mountain Meadows was ahead of them.

And those that were in Beaver were not massacred?

No; but two of them were shot in Beaver, but
not killed.

By whom were they shot, if you know?

By the Indians.

Did the Indians point out to you, or tell you on your journey, where any of these poisoned springs were?

Yes, sir.

Where were they?

On the north of Salt Creek, where the Willow Creek is now.

Were there any other places?

Yes, sir; down below Fillmore, between Fillmore and Corn Creek, at some springs down there in the bottom.

Do you know of any fatality resulting to the Indians by reason of this poisoning?

No.

Did the Indians claim of any?

No.

By what means did they tell you, if they told you at all?

They didn't tell me by what means, only they knew that the "Mericats" had done it.

Were the Indians pretty boisterous in their behavior?

Yes, sir; threatening all along through the settlements, that is what they were.

And this had caused the excitement in the community?

Yes, sir.

What, if anything, do you know concerning any orders issued to John D. Lee previous to the massacre by any one in authority?

There was an order issued to John D. Lee by Isaac C. Haight to keep the Indians in check till I came back from Salt Lake City, and that I was starting right then.

Did you see that order?

I saw that order and read it and those words were on it—I know this to be the fact.

When did you first learn of the massacre?

Not till I got home again. Never heard of it from the time I left till I got back.

You said when you gave the dispatch to Haight he read it and burst into tears and said it was too late?

Yes, sir.

Who was, to the best of your knowledge and belief, duly considering your opportunities for knowing, responsible, or held responsible, for the massacre at Mountain Meadows?

John D. Lee.

Was it by authority from anyone or upon his own responsibility.

On his own responsibility.

Is that all you know of the transaction of a material nature?

I guess that is about all.

Do these answers that you have given here embrace the sum and substance of your testimony given at the second trial of John D. Lee, in Beaver City.

That is the sum and substance of it.

Does it embrace all you gave there?

Yes, sir, and more.

TERRITORY OF UTAH, }
    County of Cache, } ss.,

Personally appeared before me, the undersignd, this 12th day of January, 1885, a Notary Public in and for said County of Cache, James H. Haslam, of said county; who, being first duly sworn, says upon his oath that the above and foregoing answers to the questions propounded to him are full, true and correct so far as his best knowledge and judgment and recollection enable him to answer the same.

JAMES HOLT HASLAM.

Subscribed and sworn to before me this 12th January, 1885.

JOSEPH HOWELL,

[SEAL.]                           Notary Public.

www.ingramcontent.com/pod-product-compliance
Lightning Source LLC
Chambersburg PA
CBHW030544270326
41927CB00008B/1507

* 9 7 8 3 7 4 3 3 9 5 7 5 6 *